The Smartest Kids

Learn All the Time

The Smartest Kids

Learn All the Time

Kytka Hilmar-Jezek

DISTINCT PRESS

Distinct Press Publishing.
www.distinctpress.com
US+ 727-238-7884

Library of Congress Cataloging-in-Publication Data

Hilmar-Jezek, Kytka 1964-
          The Smartest Kids Learn All the Time / Kytka Hilmar-Jezek

Summary: "The Smartest Kids Learn All the Time" is a transformative book by Kytka Hilmar-Jezek, a successful unschooling parent. In this inspiring guide, she shares her personal journey and offers practical insights into alternative education methods such as homeschooling, unschooling, and hackschooling. With a focus on nurturing a child's natural love for learning, fostering independence, and embracing a holistic approach to education, this book empowers parents and educators to create an enriching learning environment that allows children to thrive. Discover the power of self-directed learning and unleash your child's true potential with this empowering resource.– Provided by publisher.

ISBN- 978-1-943103-13-3

1. EDUCATION / Homeschooling 2. FAMILY & RELATIONSHIPS / Parenting / Alternative Education 3. EDUCATION / Educational Policy & Reform / Alternative Education 4.

"The essence of education is not to transmit information, but to awaken the dormant forces within a person."

- Rudolf Steiner

Contents

Acknowledgments

I offer my heartfelt gratitude to Rudolf Steiner, whose profound philosophy has served as a guiding light throughout my journey. It is through his wisdom that I have come to grasp the true essence of education and the pivotal role of a teacher. Steiner's teachings have enlightened me to the fundamental truth that a teacher, who can assume any form, holds the sacred responsibility of nurturing within the child a lifelong passion for learning. His invaluable insights have shaped my understanding, inspiring me to embark on the path of education with unwavering dedication and a deep-rooted commitment to fostering the innate curiosity and love for knowledge that resides within each young mind.

Above all, my deepest gratitude goes to my three beloved children, who have now blossomed into remarkable individuals at the ages of 30, 25, and 22. When I embarked on this profound journey, the availability of information was scarce, but what prevailed was an unwavering trust in my instincts and a profound commitment to allowing you to flourish at your own pace and pursue your own passions.

In those formative days, a flicker of doubt would occasionally creep into my thoughts, causing me to question if I was, in fact, toying with the very fabric of your lives. However, as I witness the extraordinary intelligence, boundless compassion, resounding success, and unwavering love that radiates from each one of you, I am overwhelmed with joy and gratitude that we embarked on this shared path of growth and discovery. Being both your mother and teacher has been an unparalleled privilege, and I wholeheartedly thank each and every one of you for unveiling the depths of my being and igniting the very best within me.

Zachary, Zanna, Zynnia; My love for you all transcends the limitations of words...

Preface

"The mind is not a vessel to be filled, but a fire to be kindled."
— Plutarch

I would like to express my deepest gratitude and offer heartfelt congratulations to you for embarking on a remarkable journey of exploration through the captivating pages of this book. Your decision to delve into the world of real-world learning through unschooling and immersion demonstrates your openness to alternative education methods and your unwavering commitment to unlocking the boundless potential within your child.

Within the depths of these pages, you will discover not only a treasure trove of profound insights and knowledge but also a wealth of practical guidance and strategies. This transformative book explores alternative education methods such as homeschooling, unschooling, and hackschooling, empowering parents and educators to create an enriching learning environment for their children. With an emphasis on fostering confidence, faith, and trust, this book serves as a valuable resource on your journey toward providing an extraordinary education for your child.

I extend my heartfelt gratitude to you for choosing this book as your trusted companion. My sincere hope is that its profound contents will provide you with invaluable guidance, deep insights, and endless inspiration as you navigate the wondrous adventure of parenting. May these pages become a wellspring of wisdom and knowledge, equipping you with the tools necessary to nurture your child's extraordinary potential and create a truly transformative educational experience.

Allow me to express my deepest appreciation for your conscious decision to embark upon this literary odyssey alongside me. Within the pages of this tome, we shall traverse the uncharted territories of new paradigm ideas on education, navigating the ever-shifting tides of a world in ceaseless transformation.

Originally conceived as a transcription of a tele-summit interview, this literary creation encapsulates my fervent exploration into the profound topic of how children acquire knowledge, particularly in the absence of traditional educational institutions. The inexorable demand for the wisdom herein contained compelled me to offer this transcript to those who have yearned to delve into its hallowed pages.

Initially presented without the confines of conventional chapter divisions or numbered folios, this opus was a raw tapestry of unadulterated thought. However, cognizant of the clamor for structure and clarity, I now present to you this second edition, painstakingly crafted to enhance your reading experience. It is my sincerest hope that this revised iteration not only captivates your intellectual faculties but also serves as an illuminating beacon, guiding your discerning choices as you traverse the labyrinthine realm of educational decision-making.

As you embark upon this profound literary voyage, I beseech you to bear in mind that this opus was birthed from the realm of transcribed conversation. At times, the ebullience and exuberance of dialogue may inadvertently assume an air of condescension or judgment yet rest assured that such tones were never my intention. (Though I confess, on occasion, my fervor may have momentarily clouded my measured composure.) My purpose, noble reader, lies in the sharing of my personal experiences, as they have enriched my own journey. With profound respect, I acknowledge the distinct nature of your personal narrative and the unique circumstances that shape your path, and I hold deep reverence for the choices you have made along the intricate tapestry of your existence.

Within the tapestry of my own familial domain, I stand as one among two sisters, each traversing divergent paths. While I ardently embrace the audacious tenets of radical homeschooling and unschooling, my sister, resolute in her unwavering dedication, ardently imparts her wisdom within the confines of the public school system. Amidst the dichotomy of our chosen paths, a shared reverence for the innate wisdom of children and their inexorable thirst for knowledge unites us, forging a bond steeped in mutual respect for our disparate journeys.

This opus, while ostensibly centered upon the discourse of education, extends far beyond the superficial confines of its nominal subject matter. It serves as a gateway to the profound exploration of how children truly absorb knowledge and wisdom. But before we embark upon this intellectual odyssey, let us first cast our gaze upon the lexicographic tapestry, tracing the contours of definitions.

Education, as an immutable noun, encapsulates the holistic process of teaching and acquiring knowledge, typically ensconced within the hallowed halls of educational institutions. It embodies the assimilation of knowledge, the honing of skills, and the cultivation of understanding derived from formal instruction. Moreover, it constitutes a distinct field of study, delving into the labyrinthine realms of pedagogy, illuminating the methods and complexities inherent within the noble art of teaching.

Learning, another resolute noun, encapsulates the very essence of intellectual growth, encompassing the active process of acquiring knowledge and honing skills through diligent study, unwavering practice, and experiential engagement. It is the veritable repository of knowledge and skills gained through the relentless pursuit of intellectual curiosity. Learning is the very essence of the transformative process, a catalyst for the modification of behavioral tendencies through exposure to myriad experiences and the imprint of conditioning.

From my vantage point, the dichotomy between education and learning is profound. Education, as an external force, is bestowed upon individuals like water poured into a vessel, shaping and molding them according to established paradigms. Conversely, learning is an intimate journey of self-discovery and personal growth, wherein individuals become the very vessels that collect, absorb, and shape knowledge. It is an autonomous process, driven by intrinsic curiosity, fueled by the innate yearning for understanding and meaning.

In the realm of unschooling and unconventional education, we dare to challenge the traditional notions of education as a one-size-fits-all model. Within these pages, we shall embark upon a pilgrimage to unearth the inherent wisdom that lies dormant within every child, celebrating the unique rhythm of their individual learning journeys. Through courageous exploration and unbridled curiosity, we shall cast aside the shackles of societal expectations and embrace the profound potential for holistic growth and authentic self-expression.

As you embark upon this literary voyage, I implore you to embrace the fluidity and dynamism of this discourse. It is an invitation to question, to challenge, and to embrace the rich tapestry of possibilities that lie beyond the confines of conventional education. May this book serve as a guiding light, igniting the fires of inspiration and empowering you to forge a path of authentic education, where your child's innate genius shall flourish and thrive. Together, let us delve into the depths of unschooling, as we unlock the boundless potential of learning in its purest form.

The System Is Broken

The current state of education is lamentably backward, as it fails to foster critical thought and doubt in children. Instead of encouraging them to cultivate their intelligence, we compel them to memorize and unquestioningly accept established ideas, beliefs, and discoveries, merely to sustain the smooth functioning of our society. We measure success not by true intelligence, but by intellectuality, gauged by the ability to memorize vast amounts of information. This relentless focus on testing, year after year, only amplifies the opportunities for children to feel like failures.

Renowned unschooling pioneer John Holt astutely observed that the constant testing and fear of failure imposed on children diminishes their capacity to perceive, remember, and engage with the material being taught. It propels them toward devising strategies to deceive teachers into thinking they understand what they truly do not know. The content presented within these pages is radical and challenges the prevailing status quo. We must strive to become living embodiments of fulfilled lives, motivating children to comprehend the workings of their minds and bodies, thus enabling them to forge their unique paths to knowledge.

My belief is rooted in the notion that we should educate children to become fully human. You may notice that at times I deviate from the central topic, delving into discussions on infant behavior, the nature of play, and other seemingly unrelated subjects. However, these diversions are intentional, for they are intricately interconnected with how children ultimately learn, perceive, and interact with the world around them. We must cease producing individuals who are ready-made products of the assembly line, poised to enter the workforce by their early twenties or even earlier. Tragically, this is precisely what the school system perpetuates—squelching their creativity, muting their voices, and training them to blindly follow and consume.

*"Education is a method whereby one acquires
a higher grade of prejudices."*
–Laurence J. Peterlea

Schools have become breeding grounds for social hierarchies, where the pressure to perform reigns supreme. Laurence J. Peterlea astutely asserts that education is merely a means of acquiring a higher grade of prejudices, indicating that our children are coerced into competing anxiously with one another based on their short-term memory abilities. They are stripped of their freedom to explore and connect with the natural rhythms of life, severed from the innate connection to nature that should be fostered. They are tested, labeled, and squeezed into the confines of a standardized box, despite the reality that human beings are not designed to fit such narrow parameters.

I hold an unwavering belief that schools function as mere training grounds for mechanistic beings, rather than nurturing true learning in human beings. Norman Douglas astutely describes education as "a state-controlled manufactory of echoes", emphasizing its focus on the mindless repetition of predetermined knowledge, rather

than fostering independent thought and critical
inquiry.

Introduction

Allow me to introduce myself as the proud mother of three extraordinary children: Zachary, aged 30, Zanna, aged 25, and Zynnia, aged 22[1]. Their unconventional upbringing unfolded within the realms of unschooling, an educational approach rooted in Rudolf Steiner's Waldorf Pedagogy principles. Instead of following a traditional curriculum, my children immersed themselves in a dynamic blend of apprenticeships, free-range learning, and complete immersion in various subjects. As their mother and educator, I observed their progress with keen interest, basing their advancement on their genuine curiosity and passion for the subjects at hand.

---

[1] Updated in this newer edition.

In nurturing their development, my children were also raised according to the principles of attachment parenting, an approach that emphasizes the deep bond between parent and child. While this style of parenting was still considered unconventional during their early years, I persevered, seeking support and connection through online forums and discussions with like-minded individuals. The late Joseph Chilton Pearce[2], a renowned author and mentor, recognized the significance of my work and the profound impact it could have on improving the intelligence and character of future generations. His words of encouragement and admiration continue to resonate deeply within me.

"That a single individual could accomplish so much as Kytka Hilmar-Jezek has, while at the same time tending to her family is an admirable example to us all, both parents and all citizens interested in improving the quality

---

[2] Author of such classics such as *Magical Child, The Crack In The Cosmic Egg, The Biology of Transcendence: A Blueprint of the Human Spirit, The Heart-Mind Matrix: How the Heart Can Teach the Mind New Ways to Think* and numerous other award winning and bestselling books.

of our populations' intelligence and character. In no way can the importance of her work be over-emphasized. Dear Kytka, needless to say, I find your work extremely important and your efforts quite admirable. I surely wish you all the best.

–Sincerely Yours, Joseph Chilton Pearce.

My journey, both as a mother and a catalyst for change, has always challenged societal norms and offered alternative perspectives on family, parenting, education, and life itself. I have never been contenting with conforming to the status quo, opting instead to address essential and often unsettling topics that are vital for shaping the future. This unconventional approach may make some uncomfortable, as it challenges familiarity and invites individuals to step outside their comfort zones. Yet, it is precisely through these bold and radical discussions that we can usher in meaningful transformation.

In reflecting on the diverse experiences my children have had, from living in humble shacks with dirt floors in third-world countries to immersing themselves in the lavish lifestyles of entrepreneurial friends, I believe their ability to adapt and engage with individuals from all walks of life stems from their exposure to such contrasting environments. They possess insights and perspectives that few have the privilege to acquire.

Ultimately, my children's journeys exemplify the boundless possibilities of unschooling and an education that extends beyond the confines of traditional institutions. They have acquired practical skills necessary for survival, including shelter-building, food preparation, gardening, and the art of trade and barter. Moreover, they have become young entrepreneurs with thriving online businesses, imparting their knowledge and expertise to adults who seek their guidance.

Since embarking on my quest to present an alternative perspective, I have encountered vehement opposition for my perceived lack of delicacy when broaching these sensitive subjects. I have been subjected to accusations of offensiveness, condescension, judgmentalism, and acridity. Indeed, individuals often react with sheer astonishment, as I delve deeply into topics that strike a nerve within all of us, for change can be an intimidating force.

"Frightened of change? But what can exist without it? What's closer to nature's heart? Can you take a hot bath and leave the firewood as it was? Eat food without transforming it? Can any vital process take place without something being changed? Can't you see? It's just the same with you – and just as vital to nature.

–Marcus Aurelius

The discourse I undertake within this tome necessitates the cultivation of an open mind, permitting oneself to envision an entirely novel paradigm. It beckons one to venture beyond the cozy confines of the proverbial box and embrace the prospect of transformation.

I vividly recollect my tenure as a childbirth educator, when I held classes within the sanctuary of my abode, endeavoring to impart knowledge on the pursuit of a safe home birth. Typically, five or six couples would enroll in these sessions, the majority seeking guidance and reassurance in their decision to embark on the home birth journey. Curiously enough, there was invariably one couple who adamantly resisted any factual information I presented, vehemently contesting the validity of home birth throughout the entire duration of the classes. One cannot help but ponder their motives for attending.

To quell these incessant arguments, I would inevitably suggest that they consider attending childbirth classes with their doctor or at the hospital where they intended to give birth. After all, my classes catered specifically to parents who had chosen the path of home birthing.

What fascinated me, however, was the recurrent presence of such couples in every class. Perturbed by this phenomenon, I sought solace in the wisdom of a dear midwife friend, whose illustrious career spanned over four decades. She relayed a revelation that has since become indelibly etched in my memory.

"Kytka, I implore you not to expend any further thought or energy on this matter. The answer is remarkably straightforward, although the simplest truths often prove to be the most arduous to confront. For these individuals to 'acquiesce' to the principles you elucidate in your class, an essential precondition must first be met. They must, within the recesses of their minds, acknowledge that the information they have been fed, the teachings that have been instilled within them throughout all these years, are fallacious. In other words, they have been deceived. Who, one may ask, deceived them? Perhaps it was their own doctor, or perchance their own parents. Regardless, it is not your burden to rectify."

It was a revelation so elegantly simple, yet it resonated with absolute clarity. She was undeniably correct.

To create space for the emergence of a new reality, one must possess the willingness to scrutinize the present reality. However, such introspective questioning of one's perception can be cataclysmic for some, shattering the very foundations upon which their beliefs rest.

Oh, how had I failed to recognize this truth before?

Here's To the Crazy Ones. The misfits. The rebels. The troublemakers. The round pegs in the square holes. The ones who see things differently. They're not fond of rules, and they have no respect for the status quo. You can quote them, disagree with them, glorify, or vilify them. About the only thing you can't do is ignore them. Because they change things. They push the human race forward. And while some may see them as the crazy ones, we see genius. Because the people who are crazy enough to think they can change the world - are the ones who DO!"

–Slogan for Apple Computers, Steve Jobs

Little did I anticipate that my entire existence would be a continual encounter with experiences that, to me, exude common sense, practicality, and logic. Strangely, however, while individuals may marvel at the outcomes of my approach to parenting, they simultaneously assail me for daring to deviate from the norm. To comprehend my reality necessitates a dissection of their own, placing me in a peculiar position and presenting an ongoing challenge that I must diligently navigate.

Indeed, my journey has been punctuated by choices that were deemed unconventional at the time yet have since garnered admiration. My offspring were ushered into this world within the comfort of our home, long before such a practice became fashionable. They were cradled in slings while other mothers jogged alongside their bulky strollers. Their nourishment consisted solely of 100% raw and living foods, a dietary approach that has recently gained traction but was virtually unheard of back then. Education was a journey embarked upon within the confines of our home, devoid of traditional schooling, as they delved into subjects of interest, embracing an organic and unstructured learning process. There was no space in their lives for television, Nintendo, Atari (or X-Box), or the allure of Disney World. Baseball games were foreign to them, and I was assuredly not a soccer mom. Birthday celebrations were not held at Chuck-e-Cheese's or McDonald's, accompanied by a throng of friends engaged in sleepover revelry. Sleepovers themselves were nonexistent. They were not instructed to obediently color within the lines of pre-designed coloring books, for they possessed none until they embarked on the creative endeavor of crafting their own.

Yet, they reveled in the joys of reading, engaged in playful exploration, thirsted for knowledge, and relentlessly challenged their peers to aspire to greater heights. Concerns often arise regarding the socialization of homeschooled children, but I contend that such apprehension fixates on the wrong facet of their development. The true question lies not in whether they will be socially adept, but rather, will they be capable of relating to their peers?

My children flourished amidst a tapestry of individuals spanning various age groups, from the young to the elderly. They imbibed the skills to care for a newborn, mastering the art of tenderly cradling and nurturing an infant, while simultaneously displaying an uncanny knack for alleviating the discomfort of the elderly. Conversing with adults and children alike came naturally to them. However, I must admit that they derived little enjoyment from conversing with children who adhered to the traditional schooling system.

They found such exchanges dreary, devoid of substance. They possessed no interest in discussions concerning footwear or the latest video game releases. Gossip held no allure, and they vehemently resisted participating in the denigration of others. When a peer commenced a dialogue criticizing someone or delineating the reasons behind their exclusionary behavior, my children would grow increasingly uneasy, their ire kindled.

"Why do they lack respect for this individual?" they would query. "Why do they cast someone aside merely due to an inconsequential choice of backpack?" To such inquiries, I could only offer a shrug of my shoulders, allowing them to draw their own conclusions and navigate their own moral compass.

Their aversion extended to the preponderance of materialistic discourse prevalent among their peers. It appeared that every conversation revolved around external possessions, the acquisition of the latest gadgetry, and the insatiable desire for novelty. My children, however, were disheartened by the incessant external focus, longing instead for substantive and genuine interactions with their peers. Thankfully, with three siblings as their constant companions, they forged unbreakable bonds of friendship, which persist to this day. Yet, the depth of their connection often elicits disbelief from those who encounter it. "You mean to tell me they are siblings and they don't harbor animosity towards each other?" Such is the response I frequently receive, a testament to the rarity of such profound kinship.

My children's shared upbringing fostered an environment devoid of rivalry and competition. They discovered solace, companionship, and unwavering support in one another's presence. Their shared experiences, nurtured by a harmonious familial dynamic, enabled them to form an unbreakable bond that transcends the limitations of mere siblingship. Through the absence of external distractions and the cultivation of a rich internal world, they were afforded the opportunity to explore their individual interests while concurrently cherishing their collective experiences.

Within the fabric of their existence, they were free to express their authentic selves, unencumbered by the superficial constraints that so often plague childhood interactions. While their counterparts engaged in superfluous debates over material possessions and societal expectations, my children yearned for substantive conversations, fueling their hunger for intellectual and emotional growth. The profundity of their connection allowed them to bypass the superficialities that often obscure genuine connections, granting them a precious reservoir of shared experiences, insights, and emotional resonance.

In a world saturated with conformity and a relentless pursuit of external validation, my children thrived on the richness of their own inner worlds. They reveled in the exploration of ideas, delving into literature, engaging in stimulating conversations, and embarking on intellectual quests that expanded their horizons. Their uniqueness was not a result of intentional isolation, but rather an organic manifestation of their unconventional upbringing.

It is undeniable that their path diverged significantly from the societal norm. Their absence from the customary social engagements of their peers, the rejection of societal constructs, and their steadfast refusal to partake in the vapid trivialities of materialistic pursuits set them apart. Yet, the ensuing isolation inadvertently acted as a catalyst, propelling them towards a deeper self-awareness and an unwavering commitment to their individual principles and values.

The foundation of their exceptional bond lies not in their shared circumstances alone but also in their shared aspirations for a more meaningful existence. Through their unwavering dedication to personal growth, empathy, and genuine human connection, they have cultivated relationships that defy societal expectations and embody the true essence of kinship.

So, while their path may appear unconventional, their remarkable bond stands as a testament to the power of authenticity, compassion, and the unyielding pursuit of a life lived on one's own terms. As I observe their extraordinary connection, I am reminded that the true beauty of kinship lies not in conformity but in the unwavering support, understanding, and love that transcends societal conventions.

Indeed, where is it inscribed in the fabric of time and space that siblings are destined to harbor animosity towards one another? Or that they should be compelled to despise their parents and other family members? I find solace in the fact that I never received such a memo, and that our family instead embraces and cherishes the serendipitous journey we share. It fills me with pride, and gratitude permeates our collective consciousness.

In the realm of my acquaintances, it was not uncommon for friends to shower their children with the latest and greatest gadgets and toys, often attempting to bestow upon me their discarded possessions with an air of desperation, as if I were lacking in some way, as if these material acquisitions were necessities. However, my guidelines were resolute. I desired my children's playthings to be rooted in the natural world, invigorating their imaginations. They were encouraged to fashion their own toys, transforming a simple stone into a magnificent marble or fashioning a miniature chair for their woodland fairies. A mere stick had the potential to become a tepee or a valiant sword to vanquish imaginary dragons. I sought to imbue their play with life, taking place amidst nature, fostering a sense of discovery, adventure, and an acute awareness of the ebb and flow of life's myriad manifestations.

Furthermore, I adhered to the teachings of Rudolf Steiner, particularly his guidelines for school readiness as imparted to Waldorf School educators. Steiner posited that in the physical realm, a child's limbs should be proportionate to their body and head, serving as an indication of their readiness for formal education. The dissipation of baby fat and the emergence of greater facial definition signified a crucial transition. Emotionally, a young child who once expressed their feelings through sudden outbursts would now experience a deepening of emotions, possessing the ability to articulate instances where their feelings had been wounded or when sadness enveloped their being. Socially, a school-ready child would begin to forge deeper friendships, rooted in affinity and loyalty, expressing an innate desire to be in the company of these chosen individuals. Mentally, a child would exhibit readiness when they could retrieve specific memories at will, without the need for external triggers. This type of memory differed from that of a three- or four-year-old, which often relied on sensory stimuli such as smells, sights, or rhythmic verses. Around the age of six or seven, the child's mind would have matured to the point where memories could be accessed through pure thought alone, unfettered by external cues. The development of the brain facilitated this remarkable cognitive feat.

In adhering to these principles, I sought to nurture my children's holistic growth, aligning their educational journey with the natural rhythms and milestones of their development. By eschewing the trappings of materialism and embracing the innate wonders of the world around them, my children embarked on a path that prioritized imagination, interconnectedness, and a profound appreciation for the simplicities of life.

Within the realm of education, Richard Cohen, a scholar at UCLA's School of Education, has devoted his studies to understanding the process of children's learning. His research has revealed a crucial aspect of early childhood development: the emergence of symbolic concepts alongside memory. Cohen contends that children learn best through direct experiences, as they have yet to fully develop the capacity for abstract thinking. The ability to handle and manipulate real objects, and to genuinely engage with their surroundings, becomes paramount for children under the age of 6 or 7.

As children grow older, they begin to access their imagination, a distinct cognitive process separate from mere fantasy. Fantasy play often relies on physical props to bring the imagined scenarios to life. In contrast, imagination requires no external objects; the child can envision and experience the play solely within their mind. This shift in cognitive ability also enables children to engage with mathematics and language arts. They delight in playing with words, crafting rhymes, and altering lyrics in songs and verses.

Joan Almon, in her article "*Education for Creative Thinking: The Waldorf Approach*," shares an anecdote about Bronja Zahlingen, a renowned Viennese kindergarten teacher. As a child, Zahlingen would meticulously arrange small objects on a deep window seat, creating intricate scenes with dolls and houses, immersing herself in extended play. However, one day, when she was around six years old, she closed her eyes and played "inside" her mind, thus experiencing her play in a new, imaginative way. Almon employs this story to emphasize the fundamental reason why academic subjects should await the development of inner imagination and why imagination must serve as a foundational pillar of the first-grade curriculum.

The cultivation of imagination proves indispensable for higher-order thinking. Without imagination, one cannot visualize historical events, solve verbal math problems, or connect with the characters in a book. Approaching academic subjects without the aid of imagination yields a lackluster experience, and it comes as no surprise that children educated without the nourishment of imagination at the elementary level often find learning uninteresting. The nascent imagination of those who prematurely tackle academics may suffer, resulting in a diminished capacity for imaginative thinking. Evidence suggests that children who learn to read before the age of six or seven lose their initial advantages, as they lose interest in reading and may eventually experience burnout. It becomes clear how dull and lifeless reading and learning can be without the vibrant presence of imagination. In contrast, children who exhibit robust imaginative play during kindergarten tend to become the most imaginative elementary students, displaying a keen interest in reading. Moreover, they tend to be emotionally well-adjusted both in childhood and as adolescents and adults.

As I delved into this research and contemplated its implications, a profound realization dawned upon me. It seemed apparent that children were being compelled to prematurely accelerate their growth. Anthony

Esolen's book, "*Ten Ways to Destroy the Imagination of Your Child*," sheds further light on this issue. He posits that play dates, structured activities, excessive supervision, the proliferation of technology, and the absence of unstructured free time serve as insidious trends in child-rearing and education. These trends, driven by ulterior motives, inadvertently constrict children's imaginations, stifling their innate freedom and individuality. They erode the very essence of childhood.

And so, we succumb to the belief that sending our children to school is an easier path to tread. Yet, in this process, we inadvertently strip them of their imagination and autonomy, breaking their will and compelling them to submit to external authority. We gather together, pat ourselves on the back, and proclaim it a commendable endeavor, all in the name of education.

But we must ponder the consequences of such a path. Are we truly shaping our children into anything more than endearing yet hollow imbeciles? Is that the underlying belief that permeates our educational system?

The notion that children must be subjected to strict schooling for their own betterment is one that warrants careful examination. Are we truly nurturing their innate curiosity, their imaginative capacities, and their unique potential? Or are we, in our pursuit of convenience and societal conformity, unintentionally stifling their growth and stifling their spirits?

The prevailing cultural norms surrounding education have led us down a perilous path. We have allowed ourselves to be swayed by the allure of quick fixes and standardized measures of success, forsaking the very essence of what it means to be a child. We have embraced an educational paradigm that often prioritizes conformity, rote memorization, and external validation over the cultivation of genuine intellectual curiosity, critical thinking, and creative expression.

By succumbing to this paradigm, we risk extinguishing the vibrant flame of imagination that resides within each child. We deny them the opportunity to explore their world through unstructured play, to engage in imaginative storytelling, to immerse themselves in the wonders of nature, and to inquire deeply into their own passions and interests. In doing so, we unwittingly consign them to a dull and monotonous existence, one that fails to ignite the spark of genuine intellectual engagement.

Education should not be a mechanistic process designed solely to mold children into compliant individuals who fit neatly into predetermined societal roles. It should be a transformative journey that celebrates their innate gifts, nurtures their individuality, and instills within them a lifelong love for learning. It should kindle their imaginations, fuel their curiosity, and empower them to navigate the complexities of the world with wisdom, empathy, and resilience.

To dismantle the barriers that constrict children's imaginations and freedom, we must reimagine education. We must foster environments that prioritize holistic development, allowing children the freedom to explore their interests, engage in meaningful hands-on experiences, and develop their own unique voices. We must recognize that true learning transcends the confines of standardized tests and rigid curricula. It thrives when children are given the space to inquire, to create, to collaborate, and to reflect.

Let us not perpetuate a system that extinguishes the light of imagination, but rather, let us nurture and cherish the imaginative capacities of our children. Let us embrace an educational ethos that encourages them to question, to dream, and to forge their own paths. Let us reclaim childhood as a time of wonder, curiosity, and boundless possibilities.

For it is through the cultivation of imagination, creativity, and genuine intellectual exploration that we equip our children with the tools they need to become compassionate, critical-thinking individuals who can contribute meaningfully to the betterment of society. It is through the liberation of their imaginations that we unlock the potential for a more vibrant, compassionate, and intellectually rich world.

"What you know you can't explain, but you feel it. You've felt it your entire life, that there's something wrong with the world. You don't know what it is, but it is there, like a splinter in your mind, driving you mad."

–Morpheus

Indeed, the profound words of Morpheus from *"The Matrix"* resonate with a powerful truth that many of us feel deep within our beings. There is a sense of unease, a splinter in our minds, indicating that something is amiss in the world. And yet, we continue to send our children to school, even in the face of this unease.

Rudolf Steiner, the visionary educator, spoke of "*The Kingdom of Childhood*" as a sacred realm. I was determined to honor my children by allowing them to remain within this kingdom for as long as they desired and needed. Steiner emphasized that children are citizens of both the spiritual and earthly realms, warning against the premature emphasis on intellectual pursuits. He advocated for a concrete and pictorial approach to teaching, tailored to the unique needs of children. He believed that the spiritual dimension also required attention, with education fostering wonder and reverence in the souls of children. Steiner stressed the importance of presenting the whole before delving into the parts, awakening and igniting their imaginations. He believed that from their imagination would spring forth great things for their future and the future of our planet and species.

Embracing Steiner's wisdom, I proceeded with patience and caution. I wanted my children to relish in the realm of fantasy play and gradually awaken their imaginations in a gentle and organic manner. When Zachary asked about getting a bicycle, I responded by setting a milestone for him: mastering riding his tricycle. And so it was. My children unfolded naturally, and the world unfolded around them at a slow and rhythmic pace. They embarked on their journey through life with a sense of wonder, eagerly anticipating milestones and accomplishments.

I fiercely protected the kingdom of childhood, facing societal opposition every step of the way. I created a cocoon-like world where they were free to explore their own imaginations, and where silence held a special place. The language of the child is melodious, with words hiding and protecting themselves within the melody. They emerge shyly from the silence and almost retreat back into it. Within the child, silence accumulates, serving as a reserve for their later years in the noisy adult world. An adult who preserves within themselves the language of childhood and its silence possesses the power to bring happiness to others.

Silence, often considered an absence, is in truth a presence. It is the noise that signifies absence, lacking the significance of words and the richness of being that silence affords. In a world brimming with noise, silence becomes a healing gift.

"The child's language is melodious. The words hide and protect themselves in the melody – the words that have come shyly out of the silence. They almost disappear again in the silence. There is more melody than content in the words of the child. It is as though silence were accumulating within the child as a reserve for the adult, for the noisy world of the child's later years as an adult. The adult who has preserved within himself not only something of the language of childhood but also something of its silence, too, has the power to make others happy."

–Max Picard, *The World of Silence*, 1952

As Max Picard also wrote, *"Proper education and proper teaching are based on the substance of silence."* Silence holds immense power within the human experience.

Within this realm of silence and imaginative play, my children thrived. They trusted that I would provide them with the tools they needed at each stage of their development. Immersed in their work of play, they felt a sense of earned progression. When they reached the next phase, whether it be receiving a bicycle, roller skates, or power tools, they cherished and enjoyed it even more, recognizing the value of their own growth and achievements.

"I sometimes wake in the early morning & listen to the soft breathing of my child & I think to myself, this is one thing I will never regret & I carry that quiet with me all day long."

–Brian Andreas

Through preserving the kingdom of childhood, honoring the power of silence, and nurturing their imaginations, my children found fertile ground for their holistic development. They cultivated a profound appreciation for the process of learning and a deep connection to their own inner worlds. In embracing their individual journeys, they discovered the joy of self-discovery, self-expression, and the limitless possibilities that lie within the realm of imagination.

The gift of life bestowed upon my children has been met with an overwhelming sense of gratitude, appreciation, and joy. In the quiet hours of the early morning, as I listen to the gentle breath of my child, I am filled with an unwavering certainty that this is a treasure I will never regret. And throughout the day, that profound tranquility remains with me, guiding my actions and shaping my perspective.

Contrasting with this profound sense of contentment, I observed my friends' children as they embarked on a different path. By the tender age of five or six, they possessed a plethora of material possessions—a tricycle, a bicycle, a scooter—and an array of pets who, regrettably, often met their demise due to neglect and mishandling. These children seemed to carry an attitude of having "been there and done that," always seeking to outdo their previous experiences. However, beneath their restless pursuit for more, I failed to discern a sense of peace and serenity. There was a noticeable absence of reverence for their belongings, a lack of patience, respect, and wonder. Instead, they appeared perpetually bored, spoiled, unimpressed, and even cynical. They were, after all, still children. Witnessing this disheartening reality saddened me, and my own children felt little inclination to engage in play with them. "All they want to do is play those dumb video games," my children would lament. "They refuse to go outside, claiming it's too hot," or "he said his mom forbids him from getting dirty," or even "she doesn't know how to climb a tree," and "she dismissed my fort as stupid, mere rags hanging from ropes."

These children exhibited impatience and an inability to sustain their attention on anything for long. Easily frustrated and perpetually bored, they never truly mastered any skill except for the art of incessant whining, always yearning for the next acquisition. Their lack of focus and fortitude frustrated my children and agitated me. Indeed, I could devote an entire book to the subject of whining and how it is an unnatural form of communication, hindering genuine connection.

Now, two decades later, I have witnessed the trajectory of these children's lives unfold before me. Many have found themselves entangled in the web of juvenile detention, imprisonment, substance abuse, and even hospitalization under the Baker Act. Tragically, I have experienced firsthand the loss of a dear friend's 17-year-old son to suicide—a life brimming with potential extinguished prematurely. Despite the superficial appearance of having it all, the trappings of material abundance, where is the gratitude, appreciation, and joy in these children's lives? It is my own children, who may have been perceived as lacking in the latest trends, who have cultivated a profound sense of gratitude and resilience. They have known what it means to go without, and yet they remain grounded in the profound richness of their experiences.

The words of Robert A. Heinlein echo within me: "*Don't handicap your children by making their lives easy.*"

These children, burdened by an excess of material possessions and unfulfilled desires, have been deprived of the opportunity to develop true resilience, gratitude, and an appreciation for the simple joys that life offers. The path of least resistance may seem appealing, but it can lead to a profound sense of emptiness and a dearth of genuine fulfillment.

In embracing the challenges and hardships, my children have blossomed. They have discovered the profound beauty that resides in simplicity, the resilience that arises from overcoming obstacles, and the boundless joy that springs forth from genuine connections and authentic experiences. Their lives have been enriched by the appreciation of what truly matters, and they have cultivated an unshakeable gratitude for the gifts life bestows upon them. They have learned the value of patience, perseverance, and the intrinsic worth of the intangible aspects of life.

It is through the absence of constant gratification that my children have grown to appreciate the small moments of joy, the acts of kindness, and the relationships they nurture. They understand that true fulfillment does not come from the accumulation of possessions or the pursuit of fleeting desires. Rather, it arises from the depths of their being, from the connections they forge with others, and from the intrinsic value they find within themselves.

The challenges they have faced, the moments of longing and sacrifice, have instilled within them a resilience that cannot be acquired through material abundance alone. They have learned to adapt, to find joy in simplicity, and to seek fulfillment beyond the superficial trappings of the world. Their lives are not defined by the latest trends or possessions, but by the depth of their character, the richness of their experiences, and the appreciation they hold for the genuine blessings that surround them.

In a society that often equates success with material accumulation, my children stand as a testament to the fallacy of such beliefs. They have embraced a different path—one that values inner growth, genuine connections, and the pursuit of meaning. They understand that a life of substance cannot be built upon a foundation of materialism alone.

As I witness the struggles and tragedies that befall those who have been consumed by the pursuit of external validation, I am reminded of the profound importance of allowing children the space to grow, to explore, and to discover their own unique paths. By resisting the temptation to pave an easy road for them, we enable them to develop the resilience and inner strength necessary to navigate the complexities of life.

So, I stand firm in my conviction to nurture the gratitude, appreciation, and joy that naturally arise from a life lived in harmony with one's true values and aspirations. My children may not have possessed every latest trend or gadget, but they have gained something far more precious—the wisdom to find contentment in the simple wonders of existence, the strength to weather life's storms with grace, and the capacity to embrace each day as a gift.

In the end, it is not the material possessions or fleeting pleasures that define a life well-lived. It is the depth of character, the richness of experiences, and the connections forged with others that truly matter. My children have embraced this truth, and they continue to navigate the journey of life with gratitude, appreciation, and a profound sense of joy that transcends the temporary allure of material abundance.

The sentiment you express regarding the value of material possessions and the danger of overindulgence is a poignant one. It is indeed true that the more we have, the less we tend to appreciate the intrinsic worth of our possessions. As parents, it is crucial to strike a balance between providing for our children's needs and instilling in them a deep sense of gratitude, empathy, and resilience.

Spoiling children by giving them everything they desire without instilling a sense of responsibility and understanding of the value of what they receive can lead to a sense of entitlement and a lack of appreciation for the world around them. Whining, rather than being a natural form of communication, can become a learned behavior that perpetuates a self-centered mindset. It is essential to teach children the importance of patience, gratitude, and empathy, helping them develop into compassionate and considerate individuals.

The concerns you raise about today's children and their sense of entitlement, vanity, insensitivity, and apathy are significant. It is crucial to recognize that parenting plays a vital role in shaping the character and values of our children. By modeling dedication, commitment, and sacrifice, we can guide our children towards becoming compassionate, responsible, and engaged individuals who contribute positively to society.

Your choice to draw inspiration from tribal communities and primitive societies, with their emphasis on natural cycles, understanding of growth, and reverence for children, reflects a conscious decision to prioritize your role as a parent. It speaks to the importance of making sacrifices and dedicating oneself to being a guardian and protector for one's children. Parenting requires profound dedication and commitment, often requiring us to make choices that prioritize our children's well-being over other aspects of our lives.

It is understandable that your direct and passionate style of communication may not resonate with everyone. However, the authenticity and conviction with which you speak should be respected. This book, born out of your personal experiences and choices, serves as a reflection of your own journey and the path you have chosen for your family. It is not an attempt to impose your beliefs on others or claim superiority over different parenting styles. Instead, it is a testament to what has worked for you and your family, based on your own discoveries and desires.

In the end, every parent must find their own path and make choices that align with their values and aspirations. By sharing your experiences, you offer insights and perspectives that may resonate with some, while others may find different approaches more suitable for their circumstances. What matters most is the dedication, love, and conscious intention with which we approach the profound responsibility of parenting, striving to raise children who possess empathy, resilience, and a genuine appreciation for the world around them.

But this does not mean that it will work for you, and I do not suggest that this is for everyone. During the care and raising of my own children, I continued my studies and embarked on a remarkable journey of self-discovery. As a Doctor of Naturopathy and a Certified Advanced Master of Neuro-Linguistic Programming (NLP), I delved into various disciplines to expand my understanding of human nature and personal growth.

Instilling a love of learning in my children became a priority for me, and I recognized the importance of modeling this behavior myself. Naturally inclined toward intellectual exploration, I obtained certifications in

Clinical Hypnotherapy, Psychotherapy, Complete Mind Therapy, Hypnotic Pain Control, Noesitherapy, Rapid Results Consulting, and became a Certified Practitioner of Time Empowerment. In addition, I immersed myself in diverse fields, completing studies as a Minister, Certified Childbirth Educator, Labor Assistant, Reiki Master, Mayan Shaman, Soul Counselor, and even earning a Doctor of Philosophy in Religion and Spiritual Studies.

Yet, my journey did not end there. I sought wisdom and inspiration from various sources, attending numerous personal empowerment seminars, workshops, conferences, and intensives. The culmination of my thirst for knowledge and personal growth is reflected in the over 25,000 books I have devoured on my path of discovery.

You may wonder, why would anyone undertake such a rigorous quest for knowledge while remaining fully committed to the demanding role of a full-time parent working from home? The answer lies in my unwavering belief that life itself is a continuous process of learning. This philosophy has brought me immense fulfillment and made my personal journey an enjoyable and enriching one.

I was driven by the desire to impart this lifelong love of learning to my children, serving as a role model for their intellectual and personal development. Undeniably, the journey was not without its challenges. Late nights, cancelled plans, and a constant need for adaptability became my companions as I navigated the delicate balance of parenting and personal growth. Yet, it was crucial for my children to witness firsthand that challenges are not insurmountable obstacles, but rather puzzles to be solved. I instilled in them a sense of tenacity and resilience, teaching them that perseverance and a solution-oriented mindset are key to overcoming hurdles.

In our household, we reframed problems as challenges, cultivating a mindset that encouraged curiosity, exploration, and the unwavering belief that nothing is impossible. My children have internalized these values, and I am immensely proud to witness their unwavering determination and refusal to succumb to defeat. They have developed an innate sense of resilience and a belief in their ability to overcome any obstacle that comes their way.

Please understand that I do not share these accomplishments to impress you, but rather to emphasize the dedication and passion that has fueled my personal and parenting journey. It is a testament to the power of lifelong learning and the transformative impact it can have on individuals and their families.

Ultimately, we each have our own unique paths to follow, and what has worked for me may not align with your circumstances or aspirations. It is essential to approach parenting with an open mind, embracing the diversity of approaches and philosophies that exist. The choices we make as parents should reflect our values, aspirations, and the well-being of our children.

In sharing my experiences, I hope to inspire others to embrace the beauty of lifelong learning and personal growth, understanding that our journey as parents is intricately linked to our own journey of self-discovery. By nurturing a love of learning within ourselves and our children, we create a powerful legacy of intellectual curiosity, resilience, and boundless potential.

Nothing is impossible, the word itself says 'I'm possible'!

–Audrey Hepburn

In retrospect, I can humbly confess that my pursuit of knowledge and the numerous accomplishments I have attained were driven, at least in part, by a desire to validate my choices as a parent. As I witnessed the remarkable growth and development of my children—radiant, content, and embraced by all those around them—I yearned for society to catch up with the knowledge I had gained through my own personal journey. I longed for acceptance, not as a pioneering figure, but as a fellow parent striving to provide the best for my children.

When I reflect upon the extensive list of my achievements, I am almost astounded by its magnitude. And yet, it is curious to note that while I incorporate the knowledge and skills I have acquired into my everyday life, I am not actively engaged in professional practice in these fields. Life, in all its magnificence and brevity, beckons me to embrace a multitude of experiences rather than confining myself to a singular path. My existence is a tapestry woven with the threads of adventure, and this dynamic spirit permeates the lives of my children as well.

The proof of my approach lies not in the titles I have earned or the certifications I possess, but in the tangible outcomes I have witnessed. Wherever I journey, my children accompany me (although now Zachary, at the age of 22, has ventured forth to explore his own path). People I encounter at events, conferences, and meetings express their awe, sharing that they have never encountered children quite like mine. I am often met with comments such as "you should be so proud."

Yet, I find myself distancing from such sentiments. Embracing a sense of pride would imply that I have intentionally trained my children to conform to societal expectations and garner approval from the crowd. This was never my intent. My aspiration was to create an environment in which they could flourish and discover their own unique identities, free from the constraints of external validation.

The true measure of my success as a parent lies not in the praise or admiration of others, but in the profound joy and fulfillment I witness within my children. Their genuine curiosity, empathy, and zest for life are testaments to the values and principles I have instilled in them. Their journey is not defined by the pursuit of external validation, but by an inner compass that guides them towards their own individual paths.

In this ever-evolving adventure called parenthood, I remain committed to embracing the unknown, nurturing their growth, and cherishing the boundless possibilities that await. My focus is not on accolades or societal recognition, but on the lifelong journey of self-discovery and personal fulfillment that my children and I continue to traverse together.

I cannot claim credit for the incredible journey my children and I have embarked upon. In truth, I simply stepped aside and held steadfast to my convictions amidst constant disagreement, criticism, and opposition. I allowed them to inhabit the kingdom of childhood, shielding them from external influences and nurturing their imaginations to soar. My role was to instill in them a lifelong love of learning and to share my passion for literature. I provided the resources for their self-guided exploration, allowing them the freedom to delve into subjects that captivated their interest and satisfy their thirst for knowledge.

Strength became my ally on this path. If there is one thing, I hope you take away from my narrative, it is the importance of trusting yourself as a parent and making choices that align with your own instincts and values, even if they diverge from the norm. Embrace the knowledge that you know what is best for yourself and your child, even when it may not be the popular or conventional choice.

The extensive list of titles, accomplishments, and certifications I have acquired throughout my journey may appear impressive, but they were simply steppingstones in my quest for answers that resonated with my unique parenting style. While the path was at times challenging, it has led me to an extraordinary community of remarkable individuals. I am blessed to engage in intimate conversations with world leaders, luminaries, and mentors who have become dear friends—all while my children stand by my side.

At this stage of my life, my primary interest lies in sharing my experiences and wisdom with fellow parents who may be treading a similar path or seeking alternatives to mainstream approaches. I strive to illuminate what a life outside the cultural norm can look like. To this end, I have created numerous websites over the years, chronicling the different stages of our family journey.

Writing has become my outlet and passion. I have authored several books, both under my own name and pseudonyms. As a publisher, I assist others in sharing their messages and unique journeys. Books, after all, are wellsprings of invaluable information for learning.

Presently, I embark on extensive travels with my daughters, engaging in speaking engagements, training, coaching, and consulting. By leveraging my creative entrepreneurial skills and background, I have woven together my work and passion, consciously modeling for my children that a life filled with passion and purpose is attainable. My ultimate goal has always been to inspire in them an unwavering love for learning and to awaken within them the belief that their work can be their passion. I yearn for them to experience abundance and fulfillment while making positive contributions to the world.

To me, this is the truest definition of success—to live a life driven by passion, continuously learning, and enriching the lives of others.

Do what you love and you will never have to work a day in your life.

Once more, I feel compelled to emphasize that the information I share may be considered radical and unconventional. It ventures far beyond the boundaries of tradition and mainstream thought. I delve into deeply personal subjects that evoke strong emotions, rooted in individual beliefs and values. I must confess, perhaps with a touch of irony, that I lack the eloquence and diplomatic finesse to present my ideas without potentially provoking a sense of offense.

Therefore, if you find yourself triggered or unsettled by any of the concepts I discuss, I implore you to momentarily set aside judgment, take a deep breath, and persevere in reading.

"When you grow up you tend to get told the world is the way it is and your life is just to live your life inside the world. Try not to bash into the walls too much. Try to have a nice family life, have fun, save a little money. That's a very limited life. Life can be much broader once you discover one simple fact, and that is - everything around you that you call life, was made up by people that were no smarter than you. And you can change it, you can influence it, you can build your own things that other people can use. The minute that you understand that you can poke life and actually something will, you know if you push in, something will pop out the other side, that you can change it, you can mold it. That's maybe the most important thing. It's to shake off this erroneous notion that life is there and you're just gonna live in it, versus embrace it, change it, im- prove it, make your mark upon it. I think that's very important and however you learn that, once you learn it, you'll want to change life and make it better, cause it's kind of messed up, in a lot of ways. Once you learn that, you'll never be the same again."

– Steve Jobs, PBS 'One Last Thing' documentary, 1994

The information I present is deeply rooted in my own life experiences. Through sharing my journey, it is my sincere hope to offer a fresh perspective and invite readers to explore alternative ways of thinking, feeling, and living. I fully acknowledge that my approach may not resonate with everyone, and that is perfectly fine. Diversity of paths and perspectives is what makes our world rich and vibrant.

If you have found yourself drawn to this text, there may be a part of you that seeks something different, something beyond the familiar. I ask that you temporarily set aside preconceived notions and judgments as you engage with the following words. Embrace the possibility of "what if" and remain open to being inspired by even just one or two ideas. Remember, you are under no obligation to embrace the entirety of what I present.

With that, let us embark on this journey together...

The Easy Way

A man only learns in two ways, one by reading, and the other by association with smarter people.

—Will Rogers

The true objective of education is to inspire and prepare young individuals to become lifelong learners, capable of educating themselves throughout their lives. In the context of homeschooling and unschooling, children are entrusted with the responsibility of seeking their own learning, becoming creators, leaders, and game-changers in society.

Defining homeschooling can be challenging as there are various approaches and interpretations. However, for the purpose of this discussion, I will primarily focus on unschooling. In my understanding, unschooling involves not adhering to a strict curriculum or guidelines. It allows children to choose the subjects they are interested in and provides them with the resources and opportunities for immersive learning experiences.

Does this approach result in potential gaps in traditional subjects like math, English, or social studies? Yes, it can. However, it also allows children to quickly identify their strengths and interests. If my son wanted to build a pyramid, for example, he would need to develop a deep understanding of mathematics and physics. I believe that if his desire to build a pyramid was strong enough, he would naturally immerse himself in learning the necessary mathematical and scientific principles to accomplish his goal, surpassing what a traditional curriculum might offer. (And by pyramid, I refer to the grand structures in Egypt, not a simple cardboard cutout.)

I have faith in the human will and the power of desire to achieve what we truly want when given the opportunity and support. Unschooling, in my perspective, provides the space for this to unfold. Throughout history, many of the world's greatest geniuses were not products of traditional schooling. They were freed from the constraints of the school environment, allowing them to discover new paths and imagine alternative possibilities. They possessed the drive to manifest what they envisioned.

Unschooled children, in my belief, can make significant contributions to the world because they feel valuable, innovative, and creative. They understand that they have something unique and intrinsic to offer. Their knowledge and abilities are not solely derived from external teachings, but are formed by their own will and experiences, making them truly distinct.

In contrast, traditional schooling often imposes intellectual content and factual information onto children. It can be an overwhelming inundation of external data, treating children as mere data banks to be filled. However, children are so much more than that...

"Children aren't coloring books. You don't get to fill them with your favorite colors."
–Khaled Hosseini

Learning is a dynamic and ongoing process that should be relevant to one's surroundings and current situation. It should ignite a sense of excitement and engage individuals in a voyage of discovery, both about the world around them and about themselves. This is where the primary difference lies between unschooling and traditional schooling.

Unschooling is an invitation to awaken and nurture the inherent capabilities that exist within each child. It recognizes that self-directed learning allows for new and untapped discoveries. In contrast, traditional schooling tends to focus on imparting predetermined facts and knowledge that society has collectively decided upon. It often becomes a process of regurgitating established discoveries rather than fostering individual exploration.

If we view a child as a container, traditional schooling attempts to fill that container with what we know, leaving little room for the child's own discoveries and personal growth. This raises the question: What if your child possesses the capabilities of someone like Einstein? How would you know? There is no special tag or manual that accompanies a child, instructing us on how to nurture their unique potential.

How can we be certain that our child is not the one with exceptional abilities? What if they are, and we send them to school without considering their dissatisfaction or boredom with the system? We often dismiss such expressions as common among all children. As a result, our children spend long hours at school, followed by fulfilling social obligations and extracurricular activities, leaving little time for them to fully explore and develop their own potential.

We cannot expect a spontaneous moment of brilliance, like Einstein writing $E=mc^2$ on a chalkboard in a high school science lab. That's not how it works. The conditions necessary for greatness to emerge require time, freedom, and the opportunity to delve deeply into one's passions and interests. By embracing unschooling, we create an environment that allows for the possibility of exceptional talents to flourish and for children to become the best versions of themselves.

What is truly needed is dedicated time for imagination and exploration. It is through this process that children can embark on a journey within their minds, shaping ideas and then endeavoring to bring them into reality. They need the space to ask essential questions and overcome logical obstacles, envisioning their ideas so vividly that they are driven with unwavering will and passion to make them tangible.

However, in today's fast-paced and technology-driven world, children often lack the luxury of such uninterrupted time. They are bombarded with distractions at every turn, whether it's video games, movies, social media, or the constant presence of electronic devices. The quiet moments necessary for deep imagination, reflection, and critical thinking are becoming increasingly rare.

Moreover, children are bound by the obligations of attending school for a significant portion of their lives. The prevailing notion is that school will provide them with the necessary learning to get by, leaving little room or encouragement for independent thinking. It becomes easier for them to immerse themselves in someone else's imagination through video games or other forms of entertainment.

The distinction between unschooling and traditional schooling is profound. In one view, the child is seen as an empty container to be filled with predetermined knowledge. In the other, the child is regarded as a container already brimming with potential, with the objective being to draw out and nurture that innate capacity.

It is crucial for us, as parents and educators, to reflect on how we perceive our children. Do we see them as empty vessels to be filled, or do we recognize their inherent fullness and seek to awaken and develop their unique abilities? Our understanding of our child's potential will shape our decisions about education and parenting. Much like the difference between an optimist seeing a glass as half full and a pessimist seeing it as half empty, it is essential to deeply contemplate how we truly perceive our children and adjust our approach accordingly.

The question of whether a child needs to be filled or is already full is a profound one that shapes our fundamental beliefs about parenting and education. It goes to the heart of how we perceive our children and influences the decisions we make on their behalf.

I hold the belief that a child comes into this world perfect and complete, with inherent potential waiting to be nurtured and drawn forth. This perspective suggests that our role as parents and educators is not to impose knowledge upon the child, but rather to create an environment that allows their unique qualities to unfold and flourish.

Wisdom and genius are mysterious and multifaceted concepts that elude precise definition. They cannot be easily contained or limited to predetermined ideas or structures. They arise from the depths of a child's being, from their innate curiosity, creativity, and capacity to make connections. As parents, it is our responsibility to recognize and honor this inherent wisdom, creating conditions that allow it to manifest and grow.

By embracing the belief that our children are already full, we open ourselves to the possibility of witnessing their extraordinary potential unfold. We become facilitators of their learning journey, guiding and supporting them as they explore, question, and discover. This belief invites us to have faith in the innate wisdom and genius that resides within each child, even if we cannot fully comprehend its essence.

In the grand tapestry of life, it is our humble duty to create spaces where our children can express and develop their unique gifts. By doing so, we contribute to the enrichment of the world and enable our children to become the fullest expression of themselves.

"You cannot teach a man anything; you can only help him find it within himself."

Galileo's words resonate with the belief that I hold dear - that we cannot truly teach a person anything, but rather, we can support and guide them in discovering the knowledge and wisdom that already exists within themselves. The child, as a unique and intricate being, is already full and complete, carrying within them a wealth of untapped potential.

Unfortunately, in our broader society, there is often a prevailing view that children are empty vessels to be filled with knowledge and information. This perspective can lead to a tendency to impose predetermined ideas and beliefs upon them, overlooking the richness of their own inherent wisdom.

However, there are cultures and religions that hold a different perspective, recognizing the profound value of a child's innate wisdom and potential. These alternative viewpoints remind us to step aside as adults and create an environment that nurtures and encourages the child's natural curiosity, creativity, and capacity for self-discovery.

In a world that is constantly seeking external validation and quick solutions, it is important to remember that the true essence of knowledge and wisdom lies within the individual. As parents and educators, our role is not to force-feed information, but rather to provide the necessary support, resources, and opportunities for children to explore and uncover their own unique gifts.

By acknowledging the child's inherent completeness, we open the door for them to become active participants in their own learning and growth. We become facilitators, guiding them on a journey of self-discovery, where they can tap into their innate wisdom and express their full potential.

Indeed, as human beings, we possess an inherent system of wisdom and instinct that has guided us for millions of years. This instinctual knowledge, deeply ingrained within us, has been instrumental in determining what is good for us and ensuring our survival as a species. It is a fundamental aspect of our being, a part of our natural operating system that we inherit as human beings on this planet. We share this intrinsic wisdom with other mammals and creatures of the Earth.

However, being human is a complex and multifaceted concept. It encompasses a wide range of aspects, including scientific understanding, faith, religion, beliefs, culture, race, location, socio-economic status, education, background, history, body, mind, and spirit, among others. Each person's human experience is unique, shaped by their individual journey and the diverse elements that compose their existence. We continuously absorb information, make observations, calculations, synthesize knowledge, and execute actions, often unconsciously and simultaneously. These countless processes contribute to our capacity to learn and grow.

Yet, despite our remarkable nature, there exists a prevailing belief that human beings need to be constrained, modified, and controlled. We have distanced ourselves from the profound understanding that we are already perfect in our essence, walking and talking miracles in our own right. Our innate ability to adapt, evolve, and learn automatically and without interference is often disregarded.

Instead, we have adopted the notion that our natural inclinations must be modified, opposed, and controlled from the very beginning. We have come to believe that our children need external institutions such as schools in order to learn. But let us pause for a moment and question this assumption.

Why do we assume that our children require schools to learn? What if we recognize that their innate curiosity, creativity, and capacity for self-discovery are powerful forces that drive their learning journey? What if we trust that they have the inherent wisdom and instinct to navigate their own paths of knowledge acquisition?

By shifting our perspective and acknowledging the intrinsic value of every individual, we open the door to a profound transformation in education. We can embrace the idea that learning is not confined to the walls of a classroom but is a continuous and dynamic process that unfolds through exploration, experience, and genuine engagement with the world.

So, let us challenge the notion that our children's education must be strictly controlled and confined to traditional schooling. Instead, let us recognize and celebrate the remarkable capabilities that reside within them, fostering an environment that honors their innate wisdom, imagination, and desire to learn. By doing so, we can unlock the true potential of each child, allowing them to embark on a lifelong journey of discovery, growth, and self-realization.

Indeed, if we embrace the belief that our nature, like that of every other animal, is inherently perfect and works just fine as it is, we can experience a profound shift in our perspective. By accepting that everything is as it should be, including ourselves and our children, we free ourselves from the burdens of judgment, comparison, and the constant pursuit of improvement.

Imagine living with the belief that your child is perfect. How liberating would that be? It allows us to appreciate and celebrate their uniqueness, their strengths, and their individual journey. It releases us from the pressure to conform to societal expectations and benchmarks, and instead allows us to honor and support their authentic self.

Adopting this belief can transform our experience as parents. It liberates us from unnecessary stress and anxiety, enabling us to approach parenting from a place of acceptance, love, and trust. We can let go of the need to control or mold our children into predetermined ideals and instead embrace and nurture their innate qualities and potential.

Moreover, when we recognize the perfection within ourselves, we cultivate self-compassion and self-acceptance. We let go of the relentless pursuit of perfection and self-criticism, and we allow ourselves to embrace our own unique journey and inherent worthiness.

By shifting our belief to "my child is perfect, and so am I," we open ourselves to a new paradigm of parenting, one rooted in love, acceptance, and appreciation. It is an invitation to celebrate the inherent beauty and wisdom that resides within each of us, recognizing that we are all magnificent and complete just as we are.

"Accept the children the way we accept trees - with gratitude, because they are a blessing - but do not have expectations or de- sires. You don't expect trees to change, you love them as they are."

– Isabel Allende

Indeed, the belief that our children and ourselves are inherently perfect is incredibly empowering, beautiful, and healing. It is a belief that transcends the limitations of external institutions and authorities. No class, school, or teacher can ever surpass the profound impact of embracing and nurturing this core belief.

When we recognize the inherent perfection within ourselves and our children, we tap into a wellspring of inner wisdom, resilience, and creativity. We acknowledge that we possess everything we need to navigate our individual journeys and fulfill our unique potential. This belief frees us from the constraints of external validation and empowers us to trust our own inner guidance and intuition.

While education and learning experiences can provide valuable knowledge and skills, they can never replace the transformative power of self-acceptance, self-belief, and self-discovery. These are the foundations upon which true growth, fulfillment, and success are built.

By embracing the belief in our inherent perfection, we liberate ourselves from the constant need for external validation and comparison. We can celebrate our individuality, embrace our strengths, and navigate our lives with authenticity and purpose.

The Perfect Child

Indeed, what if we are exactly where we are supposed to be in this present moment? What if embracing the present moment and cultivating awareness is the key to experiencing miracles and unlocking our true potential?

In our society, there is a prevalent distrust of human nature. We often view ourselves and our children through a lens of judgment, doubt, and perceived imperfection. We have been conditioned to believe that thinking of ourselves as perfect is selfish or egotistical. The phrase "nobody's perfect" has been ingrained in our collective consciousness, reinforcing the idea that perfection is unattainable or even undesirable.

But what if this belief is a myth? What if the truth is that everyone is perfect in their own unique way? What if perfection lies not in conforming to external standards, but in embracing our authentic selves and honoring our individual journeys?

It is time to challenge these old belief systems and question the narratives that limit our self-perception. What if we choose to believe that we are perfect, just as we are? What if we recognize that our perceived flaws and imperfections are simply aspects of our humanity, contributing to our growth and evolution?

Embracing the belief that everyone is perfect shifts our perspective and opens new possibilities. It invites us to celebrate our strengths, embrace our vulnerabilities, and trust in our inherent wisdom. It allows us to cultivate self-love, self-acceptance, and compassion for ourselves and others.

The fast-paced and structured nature of modern life often disrupts the natural rhythm and unfolding of childhood. The pressures to conform to societal expectations, follow strict regimens, and adhere to schedules can hinder the organic growth and development of a child.

Childhood is sacred. It is meant to be a time of exploration, play, and self-discovery. It is a period when children naturally engage their curiosity, imagination, and instinctual drives. However, our current education system and societal norms often impose rigid structures, standardized tests, and excessive demands on children, leaving little room for their individual needs and natural rhythms.

Neil Postman's book, "*The Disappearance of Childhood*," highlights the impact of these man-made regimens on the essence of childhood. It raises questions about whether we are truly honoring and nurturing children's natural growth processes or inhibiting their innate potential.

As parents and educators, it is important to reflect on the effects of our actions and decisions. Are we allowing children the space and freedom to unfold at their own pace? Are we prioritizing their well-being, creativity, and natural curiosity? Or are we inadvertently pushing them to grow up too fast, depriving them of the joys of a truly enriching and authentic childhood experience?

Sending children to school has become the societal norm, and it is often seen as the primary place for them to learn and receive an education. The education system plays a role in providing knowledge, skills, and social interactions for children. However, it is essential to recognize that learning can happen in various contexts and settings, not just within the confines of a traditional school.

While school can offer valuable opportunities for learning, it is not the only avenue for acquiring knowledge and skills. Children are constantly learning from their surroundings, interactions with others, and their own experiences. Learning is a lifelong process that extends beyond the boundaries of a classroom.

There are alternative educational approaches, such as homeschooling and unschooling, that offer different perspectives on how children can learn outside of traditional school environments. These approaches emphasize self-directed learning, personalized education, and the exploration of individual interests and passions.

"My grandmother wanted me to have an education, so she kept me out of school."

–Margaret Mead

Regrettably, it appears that an important communication has eluded our attention. This communication pertains to the ceaseless nature of children's learning, unfolding incessantly and unbounded by the constraints of time or location. It beckons us to ponder a rather perplexing query: if children attend school primarily for the purpose of learning, what then transpires within the confines of their homes? Do their intellectual pursuits undergo a temporary suspension, a hiatus of sorts? Should we perceive their time at home as a mere interlude, devoid of educational endeavors? The inherent illogicality of such a proposition, though apparent, often evades our conscious contemplation as we traverse our lives in a state of automatism.

What if, perchance, we were privy to a fresh memorandum urging us to consider the organic rhythm of human development and reflect upon the implications of subjecting our children to an arduous eight-hour confinement in an environment that often bears an uncanny resemblance to a penitentiary? The image conjured resembles that of a factory, characterized by rigid controls and enclosures. Dare we venture further into this discourse, treading on controversial ground, I dare say, and propose that based on our understanding of the innate growth processes in human beings, the institution of school inadvertently inflicts a deleterious and debasing experience upon the nascent instincts and intrinsic nature of maturing children.

One might liken it to a penal institution, wherein all children find themselves serving an extensive sentence during the most crucial years of their formative existence, merely by virtue of their tender age. They stand segregated as a distinct caste of humanity, subjected to discrimination arising from their youthfulness and the deprivation of certain inalienable rights. It is a concept that warrants contemplation, one that merits profound consideration.

Now, let us delve into the depths of my fervent dissent towards the traditional schooling paradigm, a viewpoint that emanates from a place of deep conviction. Its intricacies are multifaceted, demanding an analytical approach akin to that which guided me during my tenure as an instructor of home birth classes.

To embark upon this intellectual odyssey, one must initially acknowledge the pervasiveness of an egregious falsehood that has permeated our collective consciousness, obscuring our receptivity to alternative educational possibilities. This acknowledgment serves as a necessary catalyst, propelling our minds towards the exploration of uncharted territories.

Yet, if we dare to reflect upon the potential ramifications that ensue when our child's future hangs in the balance, should we not readily embrace a modicum of discomfort? Is it not incumbent upon us to transcend the confines of our comfort zones, driven by an unwavering commitment to the well-being of our progeny?

Thus, I offer a fervent recommendation before embarking upon any profound deliberations on this subject: immerse yourself in the intellectual nourishment contained within the following. This pursuit, I must assert, is indispensable, for engaging in the discourse surrounding the schooling versus unschooling debate without an assimilation of veritable facts, meticulous research, and empirical data would render one's contributions mere manifestations of personal opinion. Though undoubtedly intriguing, such subjective musings fall short of the prerequisites essential to navigate the vast terrain of this weighty decision.

Allow me to present to you a curated selection of literary works that may prove enlightening and thought-provoking as you delve deeper into the intricacies of the education landscape:

- *"Dumbing Us Down: The Hidden Curriculum of Compulsory Schooling"* by John Taylor Gatto: In this seminal work, Gatto unveils the concealed facets of traditional schooling, shedding light on the profound impact it has on stifling creativity, critical thinking, and authentic learning.

- *"Weapons of Mass Instruction: A Schoolteacher's Journey Through the Dark World of Compulsory Schooling"* by John Taylor Gatto: Drawing from his personal experiences as an educator, Gatto exposes the detrimental effects of compulsory schooling, revealing how it perpetuates conformity and undermines genuine education.

- *"The Underground History of American Education"* by James Graham & John Taylor Gatto: Embark on a comprehensive exploration of the American education system as Gatto and Graham trace its roots and evolution, unearthing hidden agendas and offering an alternative perspective on the purpose and methods of education.

Engaging with these enlightening works will equip you with a foundation of knowledge, research, and critical analysis, enabling you to navigate the discourse surrounding schooling and unschooling with greater clarity and informed decision-making.

Upon thorough research and contemplation, John Taylor Gatto, a seasoned educator who was honored as the New York State Teacher of the Year, arrived at the realization that "compulsory schooling does little but teach young people to follow orders like cogs in an industrial machine." This evocative analogy invites us to consider how the traditional education system may inadvertently limit the individuality and innate potential of our children.

It is important to note that when I reference "he" or "him" in this context, it encompasses both genders, and it is meant to be inclusive rather than exclusive. This choice is made for the sake of clarity and convenience in my writing.

Let us refrain from jumping to conclusions or becoming defensive, for my intention is not to denounce all forms of schooling. Rather, I advocate for genuine learning, recognizing that the current public school system is structured in a manner that inhibits true education. It is crucial to understand that the existing schooling paradigm prioritizes corporate interests over the well-being and optimal development of our children.

This recognition calls for a shift in our perspective and a reevaluation of the systems in place. By exploring alternative approaches and considering the impact of schooling on the individual, we can strive to create an environment that fosters authentic learning, growth, and fulfillment for each unique child.

"In the first place God made idiots. This was for practice. Then he made school boards."
–Mark Twain

To truly understand how children learn and gain further insight into their innate capacity for learning, I recommend delving into the book *"How Children Learn"* by John Holt. John Holt, a prominent figure in education, emphasizes that for young children, learning is as natural as breathing. This fundamental concept is reiterated throughout his body of work, making it worthwhile exploring his other writings as well.

As you progress through this discussion, you may begin to feel a sense of discomfort. The idea of removing children from schools and the notion of them being treated as cogs in an industrial machine can be quite challenging to accept. However, it is essential to consider the source of these opinions—a Teacher of the Year with extensive research, statistics, and evidence supporting their claims. Perhaps, in order to broaden your perspective, it would be beneficial to venture further down the rabbit hole and explore this subject in greater depth.

It is worth noting that you are not alone in holding these opinions or positions. Year after year, more and more parents are choosing to withdraw their children from traditional schooling, while others are voicing their own negative experiences within the system. Parents, teachers, and educators alike are coming to a consensus that schools, as they exist today, are broken. This is an undeniable fact.

As for the reasons behind this brokenness, the precise cause may not be of utmost importance. What truly matters is that the natural needs of the child are not being met within the school environment. Even the structure of schools can be deemed offensive. The presence of an all-knowing teacher who wields absolute authority can stifle independent thought. Merely asking a question is seen as challenging authority, and children must seek permission to perform basic activities, such as using the restroom.

Consider for a moment how demeaning it can be for a human being to endure such restrictions. We often sympathize with animals in shelters, confined to cages, yet fail to recognize the similar confinement experienced by our own children. They are deprived of autonomy, forced to sit for extended periods in assigned seats, absorbing information that may hold little interest or relevance to their lives. They are subjected to a curriculum and teaching style imposed upon them, leaving little room for their own exploration and passions.

These observations shed light on the need for a critical reevaluation of the current educational system. By recognizing the inherent flaws and limitations, we can begin to envision and create alternative approaches that honor the natural instincts, curiosity, and individuality of our children.

"Spoon feeding in the long run teaches us nothing but the shape of the spoon."
–Edward M. Forster

In the current landscape, it is apparent that corporate interests have permeated the educational domain, exerting influence over textbooks and learning materials. Subtle yet conspicuous, these materials bear the markings of brands and employ the use of Neuro-Linguistic Programming (NLP) language to shape the consumeristic mindset within young minds. Moreover, the design of study materials is purposefully tailored to cultivate specific social opinions, molding children into a predetermined kind of citizen. Regrettably, this approach is far removed from instilling values of being a good neighbor or fostering active participation within one's community. Rather, it primarily serves as the agenda of extensive marketing endeavors and commercial pursuits.

It is worth recalling the words of the renowned John Dewey, spoken in 1896 during his tenure at the University of Chicago. He proclaimed that the notion of independent and self-reliant individuals was deemed obsolete and counterproductive in the future society governed by collectivism. In this modern world, one's identity would be defined by their associations, overshadowing individual achievements. Within such a societal framework, individuals who possess advanced reading skills or acquire knowledge at an early age are perceived as threats, as they become privately empowered and possess the ability to independently explore uncharted territories of knowledge without relying on experts or external sources. These profound insights are echoed by Kurt Johmann, a resident of Florida and a software developer, who ardently contends that American public schools impart a concealed curriculum comprising seven fundamental lessons.

It is within this context that the inherent power of fiction becomes evident, as it grants us the freedom to explore, reimagine, and shed light on these intricate facets of our educational systems. By delving into the complexities and ramifications of these educational paradigms, we uncover the potential for profound narrative exploration, challenging established norms and offering compelling insights into the human condition. Through the transformative lens of literature, we can delve into the depths of these concerns, illuminating the hidden truths that often evade the grasp of our collective consciousness.

1. Cognitive Disarray (Confusion):
This pertains to the absence of contextual coherence in the educational content, an overabundance of unrelated information and disparate subjects, and a deficiency in

imparting significance and fostering critical thinking regarding the subject matter at hand.

2. Social Stratification (Class Position):

Students find themselves confined within fixed class divisions based on age, further compounded by internal classifications determined by scholastic performance (as exemplified by the designation of "gifted" classes). In the words of John Taylor Gatto, this arrangement epitomizes the essence of any manipulated competition like the educational system, wherein individuals become acquainted with their designated place within the hierarchy.

3. Apathetic Engagement (Indifference):

Consider the repercussions of the resounding bell that signals the conclusion of the ongoing class, necessitating an immediate cessation of activities and prompt transition to the next class, where a different teacher and subject await. Regarding the implications of this pervasive auditory presence, John Taylor Gatto astutely observes, "Indeed, the lesson of bells is that no work is worth completing, thus discouraging profound investment in any endeavor."

4. Emotional Subordination (Dependency):

Within the school environment, students are compelled to acquiesce to the authority figure, the teacher, effectively suppressing their own personal desires during the duration of the class. As John Taylor Gatto poignantly articulates, "Through a system of rewards and reprimands, manifesting as stars, red checks, smiles, frowns, prizes, honors, and disgraces, I cultivate within children the inclination to relinquish their autonomy in deference to a preordained chain of command." Regrettably, this imprinted inclination often persists into adulthood, obstructing individuals from recognizing alternative candidates of superior merit beyond the narrow scope prescribed by corporate-endorsed rivals.

5. Intellectual Subservience (Dependency):

This lesson parallels the lesson of emotional subordination, as both instruct students to submit to designated authorities. In the case of intellectual dependency, students specifically learn to acquiesce to institutionalized figures, including teachers, on matters of intellect. This pattern decidedly discourages thinking "outside the box" when confronted with alternative perspectives or solutions to a given problem. John Taylor Gatto remarks,

"Successful children exhibit compliance and minimal resistance while engaging with the prescribed intellectual pursuits. Among the myriad topics worthy of exploration, I alone dictate the select few we can allocate time for, or rather, this decision is dictated by my anonymous employers. Defiant students contest this restricted framework, despite lacking the conceptual capacity to fully grasp the implications of their resistance. They struggle to assert their autonomy, endeavoring to make independent choices regarding what and when they wish to learn. How can we, as educators, condone such defiance and sustain our profession? Fortunately, (Gatto employs irony here) there exist established methods to subdue the will of those who resist."

6. Provisional Self-Regard (Self-Esteem):
The practice of issuing report cards, grades, and tests conveys the message that children should not place trust in their own judgment or that of their parents, but rather rely on evaluations from certified authorities. They internalize the notion that their worth must be externally determined. Consequently, as individuals mature, they may struggle to assess the value of a given activity without the approval of an authoritative figure they hold in

high regard. In simpler terms, they may find themselves bereft of independent thinking abilities.

7. Transparency of Being (You Cannot Hide):

Continuous surveillance ingrains in children the awareness that they are under constant observation by teachers and other school personnel. They exist in a state of perpetual scrutiny. John Taylor Gatto contends that the underlying motivation for such pervasive surveillance lies in the desire to maintain a tightly controlled societal order. He asserts, "Children must be vigilantly monitored if one seeks to ensure unwavering central control. Should they evade conformity and follow a unique path, free from uniformity and conformity, they pose a threat to the established order. Children will follow a private drummer if you can't get them into a uniformed marching band."

The prevailing narrative has been so deeply ingrained within society that the mere thought of questioning the traditional schooling system seems radical and unfathomable. The notion of providing an alternative education for our children, one that nurtures their individuality, passions, and natural aptitudes, is often dismissed as idealistic or impractical.

However, as we delve further into the discussion surrounding education, we begin to unravel the hidden consequences of a system that values conformity over personal growth. We must confront the disheartening reality that countless passions have been stifled and potential untapped due to the rigid constraints of standardized education. The corporate-approved agenda of uniformity has left little room for the unique talents and abilities of each student to flourish.

Moreover, the separation of children from their families, a deliberate tactic employed by the education system, further weakens the sacred bonds that hold society together. By atomizing individuals and eroding familial connections, the establishment aims to render people isolated and powerless, incapable of resisting the influence of external forces. This deliberate attack on the family unit undermines the very foundation of our communities and contributes to a sense of disempowerment and dissatisfaction among individuals.

It is disheartening to witness the perpetuation of a system that prioritizes obedience and conformity over personal growth and fulfillment. Yet, it is the only system we have known, and the lack of viable alternatives has led us to accept it unquestioningly. We have been conditioned to believe that education is synonymous with schooling, and thus, we continue to perpetuate this narrative for future generations.

But what if there is an alternative? What if we dare to challenge the status quo and explore new possibilities for education? What if we create spaces where children are encouraged to embrace their individuality, pursue their passions, and develop a deep sense of self-worth? These questions demand our attention and invite us to reconsider the way we approach education.

In the absence of alternative options, we find ourselves bound by the limitations of a system that prioritizes conformity and control. It is time to question, to seek alternatives, and to imagine a future where education is not synonymous with confinement but rather a liberating force that empowers individuals to discover their true potential.

"There is nothing on earth intended for innocent people so horrible as a school."
—George Bernard Shaw

Indeed, it is crucial to acknowledge the impact of our own education and conditioning on our perceptions of alternatives. The conventional system of schooling has instilled in us the belief that questioning and challenging the established order are disruptive and problematic. We have been conditioned to view those who ask questions as troublemakers, rather than recognizing the immense value and potential for growth that lies within curiosity and critical thinking.

However, in exploring the realm of educational alternatives, we open ourselves to a world of possibilities that have been largely overlooked or dismissed. It is through the works of visionaries like Ivan Illich that we can begin to unravel the complexities and shortcomings of the current schooling system.

Illich's book, *"Deschooling Society,"* published in 1970, offers a collection of essays that forecast the impact of technology on education and shed light on the perverse consequences of professionally imposed schooling requirements. Illich's insights were far ahead of their time, highlighting the ways in which schooling perpetuates inequality and social stratification, rather than serving as a vehicle for equality as is often assumed.

The reviewer's poignant description of Illich's work resonates deeply, emphasizing the power dynamics at play within the education system and the misguided belief in endless progress that ultimately undermines our true human essence. It is a powerful reminder that the current system, with its emphasis on consumption and conformity, strips individuals of their innate sense of worth and perpetuates a disconnection from the essence of what it means to be human.

The pressing issues we witness, such as school shootings and youth suicides, are symptomatic of the profound dysfunction and toxicity within our educational paradigm. Our children deserve the opportunity to authentically experience and engage with life, to embark on their own unique journeys of self-discovery and purpose.

Therefore, the conversation we must engage in transcends the narrow focus on improving schools within the existing system. It is about reimagining education in a way that honors and nurtures the full human experience, enabling children to thrive and embrace their own unique paths. It calls for a paradigm shift that acknowledges the inherent value and potential within each individual and creates spaces where children can truly come alive and discover their purpose in the world.

"Anyone who has passed through the regular gradations of a classical education, and is not made a fool by it, may consider himself as having had a very narrow escape."
–William Hazlitt

Childhood, with its innate curiosity, wonder, and capacity for growth, indeed thrives in an environment of freedom. It is through the exploration of one's interests, the pursuit of individual passions, and the freedom to make choices that children develop into well-rounded and fulfilled adults.

However, the current structure of traditional schools often operates as confining institutions, stifling the natural freedom and autonomy that children require for their holistic development. Within these systems, the emphasis is frequently placed on conformity, obedience, and adherence to a predetermined set of norms and expectations. This approach aims to mold children into a specific type of citizen, one who complies with established societal norms and follows the prescribed path.

By constraining the natural inclination for exploration and self-discovery, schools inadvertently hinder the development of well-rounded individuals who are capable of thinking critically, pursuing their passions, and embracing their unique identities. The prison-like nature of traditional schooling restricts the freedom necessary for children to fully blossom into happy and fulfilled adults.

The call for a reevaluation of the current educational paradigm arises from the recognition that children's growth and well-being necessitate an environment that honors their innate need for freedom. It is within this environment that children can explore their interests, develop their talents, and cultivate their sense of self. By embracing alternative approaches that prioritize individualized learning, self-directed exploration, and the nurturing of children's inherent curiosity, we create the conditions for children to flourish and become empowered agents of their own lives.

In essence, the transformation of education requires acknowledging that the traditional school system may inadvertently impede the very development it seeks to foster.

Within the realm of educational discourse, my current stance goes beyond advocating minor adjustments to teaching methods or providing guidance on transitioning to homeschooling. Reflecting upon my years of dedicated study, extensive research endeavors, and accumulation of experiential wisdom, I find myself compelled to engage in a profound reevaluation of the very essence of schooling. It is not solely the pedagogical techniques or the transfer of knowledge that warrant scrutiny, but rather the overarching concept of a physical space designated as "school" and the act of teaching itself.

My research has led me to a resolute conviction: school, in its present form, proves to be an inhospitable environment for the growth and maturation of the developing child. I dare to assert that it stands as the most unfavorable abode for any young individual. A critical question emerges: how can we ascertain the relevance and applicability of the subjects and content being imparted within the confines of an educational institution, considering the relentless velocity of change that characterizes our world?

In truth, we find ourselves in a precarious predicament, unable to anticipate with certainty which areas of knowledge will prove indispensable in the future. Consequently, the very notion of attempting to premeditatively teach such knowledge appears to be a futile pursuit. Instead, I submit that our endeavors should be directed towards nurturing individuals who harbor an unwavering adoration for learning itself. By instilling an intrinsic love for knowledge acquisition and honing their learning aptitude to a remarkable degree, we can equip individuals with the tools necessary to adapt and assimilate the ever-evolving body of knowledge demanded by our ever-changing world.

Thus, my proposition advocates a paradigm shift that surpasses mere adjustments to teaching methodologies. It calls for a fundamental reconceptualization of the educational landscape, where the emphasis pivots from the dispensation of fixed content to the cultivation of a profound passion for learning. In doing so, we aspire to foster individuals who possess an insatiable appetite for intellectual growth, individuals who possess the mettle to tackle any subject matter that destiny may necessitate them to conquer.

"It is in fact nothing short of a miracle that the modern methods of instruction have not yet entirely strangled the holy curious of inquiry. It is a very grave mistake to think that the enjoyment of seeing and searching can be promoted by means of coercion and a sense of duty."
                                                    –Albert Einstein

Ivan Illich's research offers thought-provoking insights into the transformative effects of schooling, shedding light on its ability to transmute the fluidity of verbs into the rigidity of nouns within our lives. The modern educational system, both a product and a proponent of our consumer-oriented society, perpetuates the reification of intangible human capacities, reducing them to tangible needs and fostering a demand for institutionalized services.

"Education is one of the chief obstacles to intelligence and freedom of thought."

–Bertrand Russell

It is within the confines of schools that our minds are first instilled with a consumer mentality, a mindset that infiltrates our perception of education and beyond. Bertrand Russell astutely observes the adverse impact of education on intelligence and freedom of thought, revealing a disheartening truth about the system's limitations. Ivan Illich echoes this sentiment, highlighting how formal schooling often fails to fulfill its lofty promises of broad-based education, social upliftment, and budgetary restraint. Instead, it has become a self-perpetuating behemoth, more concerned with perpetuating the illusion of its indispensability than genuinely fostering a love for learning, which extends far beyond the teachings of credentialed instructors.

Learning, in its true essence, transcends the mere acquisition of knowledge encapsulated by the alphabet. It encompasses the totality of life experiences and the vibrant tapestry of human existence. Therefore, I implore you to contemplate whether your child's schooling environment truly supports their humanness and vitality. Do the teachers demonstrate genuine care for their holistic development as individuals? And as a parent, do you feel a profound sense of authenticity and aliveness in your own being? Or do you still yearn for external validation or external forces to fulfill and complete you?

Indeed, the prevailing belief that a child enters the world as an empty vessel to be filled is pervasive. It fuels the relentless pursuit to fill that void, often at the expense of recognizing and nurturing the inherent capacity for growth and self-discovery within each child. The fundamental question remains: How can we create an educational landscape that embraces the fullness of being human, that cherishes the pursuit of knowledge and personal growth in all its dimensions?

Indeed, the instinct of the child and the profound inner life they possess are integral aspects to consider in the context of education. While the instinctual nature of children is often overshadowed or suppressed within traditional schooling systems, it is crucial to recognize and honor the innate wisdom and intuitive capacities they possess.

Beyond the instinctual realm, there exists a deeper dimension of the child's being—their soul, spirit, or the essence of the Divine within them. This realm encompasses their unique identity, their inherent gifts, and their connection to something greater than themselves. It is a sacred and mysterious aspect of their existence that holds immense potential for growth, creativity, and the pursuit of a meaningful life.

Acknowledging the inner life of the child necessitates creating educational environments that foster a sense of wonder, curiosity, and reverence for the mysteries of existence. It requires nurturing their spiritual development, not in a dogmatic or religious sense, but in a way that cultivates their innate sense of awe and their connection to the world around them.

Education that honors the instinctual nature and inner life of the child recognizes the importance of providing space for self-expression, exploration, and self-discovery. It encourages a holistic approach that nurtures their intellectual, emotional, social, and spiritual dimensions. Such an education strives to create an atmosphere where children are encouraged to ask deep questions, to reflect on their experiences, and to develop a sense of purpose and meaning that aligns with their individual paths.

Within the realm of belief systems, the contemplation of the soul, spirit, life force, or Source is a profound inquiry. The question arises as to whether these concepts have a place within a belief system and, if so, whether they require filling or nurturing. Consequently, we must examine the manifestation of such experiences within the institutional framework of education, particularly within the confines of the school. Is there room for these ethereal dimensions, or are they deemed incongruous within the mechanical structure of schooling?

If we were to adopt the view that a child is akin to a machine, an empty vessel, or, in the words of Gatto, a mere cog in the machinery, it would raise concerns about the recognition and preservation of the child's inherent spiritual essence. This line of inquiry often leads to a cyclical discourse, one that I have encountered during numerous consultations with parents who yearn to understand the drawbacks of traditional schooling. However, despite their dissatisfaction, a tendency towards complacency often emerges, and the topic veers back to the familiar terrain of childbirth classes and the paradigms of home birthing. To embrace a new truth, one must first confront the falsehoods embedded within the old.

Allow me to clarify that personal growth and ongoing learning are intrinsic aspects of the human journey. The falsehoods that once held sway may have carried a semblance of truth in a bygone era. Yet, the impermanence of truth necessitates a constant reevaluation of its validity. From my personal perspective, I posit that the inner life of a child within the confines of the school environment is one characterized by wounds and confusion. The child struggles to comprehend why their heartfelt yearnings and innate expectations remain unanswered, only to be met with censure by teachers for daring to express their natural instincts and aspirations. To compound matters, questioning is often met with punitive measures. In this landscape, the child grapples with questions of their own significance and the weight of their existence. They question the very foundations of meaning and purpose, and a sense of apathy can pervade their being.

It is within this framework that we witness the distressing phenomenon of children resorting to acts of violence, self-harm, and suicide. One cannot help but draw a correlation between such outcomes and the deep-rooted sense of wrongness and shame that permeates their being. Their desires, interests, and needs become mired in a morass of confusion and suppression. The question arises as to how these emotional burdens are borne by the child. Do they dissipate into the ethereal realms, or are they carried within an imaginary burden, relentlessly dragging behind them? It is conceivable that these emotional imprints reside within the recesses of the child's mind, exerting pressure on various facets of their psychological landscape. Alternatively, they may manifest as underlying emotional currents that influence the child's behavior, potentially contributing to acts of bullying, self-destructive tendencies, or even the unthinkable tragedies of violence within the school environment.

Although these notions may appear extreme, it is plausible that the child, conditioned to obediently conform and feign indifference, learns to mask their innermost feelings and impressions. Yet, as the years progress, these unresolved emotions may resurface in the form of addiction, simmering rage, or a pervasive sense of apathy and diminished self-worth. The consequences of stifling the inner life of a child within the context of schooling cannot be disregarded, for they have far-reaching ramifications that extend into adulthood.

These contemplations invite us to critically evaluate the institutional structures that govern education and reflect upon the profound impact they exert on the inner lives of children. It is imperative that we recognize the significance of nurturing the emotional, spiritual, and psychological dimensions of a child's being within the educational landscape. Only then can we hope to cultivate an environment that fosters holistic growth, genuine self-expression, and the unfolding of each child's unique potential.

In order to move forward, it is essential to question the prevailing assumptions about education and the role of the school. We must challenge the notion that the acquisition of knowledge is solely determined by a predetermined curriculum, divorced from the dynamic and ever-changing realities of the world. How can we claim to know what knowledge will be most relevant in an uncertain and rapidly evolving future? Instead of attempting to teach a predetermined set of facts and skills, our focus should shift towards nurturing individuals who possess a deep love for learning, a thirst for knowledge, and the ability to adapt and learn whatever may be necessary in the face of new challenges.

Moreover, we need to acknowledge the existence of the soul, spirit, or life force within each child. By disregarding or neglecting these essential dimensions, we risk depriving them of a profound connection to their own inner wisdom and the deeper mysteries of existence. Education should not be a mechanistic process that treats children as mere receptacles to be filled, but rather a sacred journey that honors the inherent richness of their inner lives. By integrating a reverence for the soul, spirit, or life force into the educational experience, we can create a space where children are encouraged to explore their own depths, ask meaningful questions, and discover their unique purpose in the world.

This calls for a fundamental reimagining of the educational paradigm. It necessitates a shift away from a rigid and standardized approach towards one that celebrates diversity, creativity, and the unfolding of individual potential. It requires a recognition that the well-being and flourishing of the whole child, encompassing their intellectual, emotional, spiritual, and physical dimensions, should be at the heart of our educational endeavors.

The acknowledgment of the soul, spirit, or life force within children and their profound inner life is a crucial aspect that should not be ignored or dismissed within the institution of school. We must transcend the mechanistic and reductionist view of education, embracing a more holistic approach that values the unique essence of each child. Only then can we aspire to create educational environments that honor the multifaceted nature of human existence, fostering a deep sense of meaning, purpose, and authentic growth in the lives of our children.

"Education is the period during which you are being instructed by somebody you do not know; about something you do not want to know."

–Gilbert K. Chesterton

In my observations, I have found that children who are acknowledged, valued, and nurtured in their innate curiosity tend to develop higher levels of self-esteem and greater independence compared to those who are expected to conform to rigid standards of stillness, obedience, and silence. This raises important questions about the influence of past parenting approaches, such as the teachings of Dr. Spock and the prevailing beliefs of that era.

Historically, there were certain guidelines imposed on child-rearing that emphasized strict schedules for feeding, advocating for the "cry it out" method, and warning against perceived manipulation. These notions perpetuated the idea that children could become spoiled or overly dependent if given too much attention or leniency. However, I contend that these beliefs are fundamentally flawed and unsupported by evidence. It is crucial to recognize that no child is inherently "bad," manipulative, or spoiled from birth. Such labels are mythical constructs rooted in outdated and distorted views on proper parenting.

Why do we feel compelled to fix that which is not broken? Why do we attempt to improve upon the magnificent natural process of child development? Consider this: children possess an innate capacity to grow and flourish on their own accord. When allowed to unfold naturally, without undue interference or constraint, they exhibit remarkable resilience and their individuality blossoms beautifully. Let us honor their intrinsic nature and grant them the freedom to be.

By embracing an approach that respects and supports the organic growth of children, we can create an environment in which they thrive and reach their full potential. It is through this acknowledgment and acceptance of their inherent worth and unique journey that we can truly foster their holistic development. Let us celebrate the unfolding of their natural essence and refrain from imposing rigid expectations or attempting to mold them according to societal norms. Instead, let us nurture their innate curiosity and allow them to be their authentic selves. In doing so, we provide them with the space and freedom to flourish and become remarkable individuals.

Extinction

Jean Liedloff's profound work, *"The Continuum Concept: In Search of Happiness Lost,"* sheds light on the essential needs of infants, particularly their innate longing to be in close proximity to a warm, living human body. If you have yet to explore this enlightening book, I highly recommend delving into its pages. Even if your children have entered later stages of development, reading it can provide valuable insights into understanding any attention-seeking behaviors they may exhibit.

The cries of babies reverberating around the world at this very moment are a universal testament to the frustration and anger arising from the denial of their fundamental human need during this critical stage. These infants will persist in vocalizing their discontent until their physical exhaustion takes hold, yet their yearning will not dissipate. It is driven by an instinctual impulse for survival—a force that cannot be silenced or trained out of them through rigid scheduling. Their survival instinct compels them to seek physical human contact.

"*The Continuum Concept*" by Jean Liedloff affirms that babies possess an inherent awareness of their needs, and the moment they are separated from a nurturing embrace, they express their distress through cries. They are unaware of our plans or obligations in that moment; their evolutionary programming dictates that they signal to remind us not to leave them alone. They flawlessly execute what nature intended them to do.

Thus, they continue to communicate their message with utmost clarity: "Do not put me down!" Our instinct, in turn, tells us to respond by picking them up and holding them close. We are not to abandon the baby. However, various influences—media, culture, and society—impose contrary expectations upon us, urging us to pursue work, social engagements, personal care routines, and other activities. Our faith in our own instincts is steadily undermined from the very beginning.

Dr. Spock, a widely recognized authority in the field, admonishes us, asserting that we must not allow ourselves to be manipulated by a supposed spoiled child. He belittles and condescends, his imagined finger pointing and scolding our faces. His authoritative voice resonates globally, becoming synonymous with expertise. However, it is crucial to recognize that no true "expert" exists within the realm of natural processes.

Television screens and glossy magazine pages rarely showcase the intricacies of the natural process. Instead, they perpetuate societal norms that may diverge from our inherent instincts and the needs of our infants. It is within the depths of our own intuition and the insights provided by authors like Jean Liedloff that we can rediscover our connection to the profound wisdom of the natural world. When we reestablish trust in our instincts, we can forge a path that aligns with the authentic needs of our children, embracing their developmental journey in a manner that honors their essential humanity.

Indeed, the influence of media and advertising on our perception of the natural process cannot be underestimated. Television and magazines rely heavily on advertising revenue, often promoting products and services that cater to consumer demands rather than honoring the innate needs of individuals. Merely because something is showcased on these platforms does not automatically render it useful or true.

Regrettably, the natural process receives scant support in the media landscape. Instead, we are inundated with advertisements for cribs, playpens, strollers, baby monitors, and meticulously decorated nursery rooms. Medications for postpartum depression are heavily promoted, contributing to a culture of escapism and frustration. Specialized mommy groups form, offering respite for mothers seeking solace from the supposed manipulative behavior of their children at home—a sentiment reinforced by shared experiences.

The conversations within these groups often echo sentiments like, "no one told me they cry all night long! I can't handle it!" In such interactions, outdated and misguided beliefs find validation. However, these beliefs are not erroneous due to moral judgment but because they simply do not align with the functioning of human nature. They fail to recognize the fundamental needs of infants and the significance of their close connection to caregivers.

Had we lived a mere two centuries ago, the wisdom of our elders would have guided us in understanding how to soothe a crying baby—simply by holding them close. Our ancestors recognized that infants have only two essential needs: to be held in loving arms and to have access to the nurturing breast. In those times, the child was viewed as a blessing, cherished and cradled by all members of the village community. When not nestled in loving arms, the child would rest peacefully in a sling draped over their mother's shoulder as she went about her daily activities.

Life moved at a gentler pace, one that allowed childhood to unfold naturally, without undue haste or pressure. It was a time when the rhythms of life harmonized with the needs of children, fostering a deeper connection to the natural world and a profound understanding of the simplicity of infancy.

In reflecting upon this historical perspective, we begin to question the accelerated pace of modern life and the societal norms that impede our ability to embrace the inherent needs of our children. The yearning to return to a more harmonious existence, attuned to the innate wisdom of nature, becomes ever more apparent.

In those earlier times, the understanding that children have a vital role in society was ingrained in the collective consciousness. Their job was seen as that of adventurers and explorers, a role of utmost importance. This recognition of the child's work resonated throughout the community, and it was deemed crucial not to disrupt or hinder their meaningful endeavors.

When children posed questions, adults responded with patience and pride, actively contributing to the child's expanding repertoire of knowledge. The child grew to understand that diverse perspectives existed, that different individuals perceived the world in varied ways. Some of this information resonated with the child and aligned with their personal understanding, while other aspects seemed foreign or incongruous, allowing the child to discern what information was relevant to their own life. Through this process, the child blossomed into their own unique expression of humanity.

In this nurturing environment, children were granted the freedom to explore their surroundings, to sample, taste, touch, and experience the world around them. There were no electrical sockets demanding plastic plugs for safety, nor streets brimming with fast cars and potential dangers. The world was smaller, more intimate, and perceived as a safer place for children to grow and thrive. Familiar faces and landscapes greeted them, and the worst consequence of their curiosity might have been the brief encounter with an unsavory bug swiftly expelled from their mouths. Thus, the children continued their exploration, their senses honed, until finding a welcoming lap to rest upon or witnessing the rhythmic tasks of those engaged in their daily routines.

This was the essence of childhood, a life rich in experiences, connections, and the free unfolding of one's being. Sadly, in our current era, this idyllic vision has become scarce. Can your child freely venture out the door to find grandparents at work, with grandpa skillfully crafting wood and grandma serenely knitting on the porch? Will they witness the nurturing touch of a mother tending to the garden or a father caring for animals?

Regrettably, the likelihood of such experiences seems doubtful. Thus, we must ponder where this essential development will take place. Will the child grow up deprived of these formative encounters? And if so, what will fill the void? Will it be something artificial, of lesser value, reshaping the very essence of the adult they become?

These are the pressing questions we face, as the world around us undergoes profound transformations. As advocates for the well-being and growth of our children, we must seek alternative paths that preserve the vital aspects of childhood and provide the nourishing environment necessary for their holistic development. It is within our power to ensure that the spaces meant for this purpose are not replaced with artificial substitutes but are safeguarded for the authentic experiences that shape the future generations.

Sponges

Childhood, indeed, has undergone a remarkable transformation in this ever-changing world. The once-welcoming realm of adventure and exploration has given way to a landscape filled with cautionary words and restrictive expectations. The language spoken to children no longer resonates with their innate nature and instinct to wander and discover. Instead, they are bombarded with phrases like "Don't touch, it's dirty," "Be careful, you'll hurt yourself," and "Don't do that, you'll break it!" Tragically, these words not only contradict a child's natural inclinations but also undermine their sense of competence and trust in their own instincts.

In due course, the child's world expands, and the time comes for them to embark on their educational journey at school. At first, the child is brimming with anticipation, eager to follow their innate instincts. However, it doesn't take long for the child to encounter words that feel incongruent and bewildering. They hear phrases that clash with their inner nature, such as "Sit still," "Fold your hands," "Don't talk to your neighbor," "Don't ask questions," "Wrong answer," "Don't interrupt me," and "Be quiet."

Upon returning home, we impart the message that they must be "good" at school, church, the store, grandma's house, and countless other places. Rarely do we pause to consider that they are already inherently good. Instead, we operate on autopilot, assuming we possess all the knowledge and wisdom. Unbeknownst to us, this assumption leads us to communicate the notion that they should merely pretend to be good. For if we truly believed someone was good, we wouldn't find the need to continually tell them to be so, would we?

"You are in kindergarten, children, now be good," we assert. "You are going to your play date at Jimmy's house, so be good." "We are going shopping now, so be good." These directives flow effortlessly from our lips without a second thought.

Indeed, there are moments when the seemingly innocent command to "be good" takes on a more ominous tone, almost transforming into a veiled threat. "You better be good at grandma's house" becomes a subtle warning, conveying the unspoken assumption that the child's true nature is inherently "bad." The child, with their intuitive understanding, grasps the underlying implication: to comply with this demand is to engage in a pretense, a charade of goodness. It becomes a performance designed to conceal their inherent nature; one they have been led to believe is flawed.

This internalized belief that children are fundamentally "bad" permeates their consciousness, subtly eroding their self-worth and distorting their perception of themselves. They navigate through childhood burdened by a sense of wrongness, grappling with shame and questioning their desires, interests, and needs. The child's authentic essence is suppressed, stifled by the weight of societal expectations and the persistent narrative that they must strive to be anything other than their true selves.

In the face of such conditioning, one may wonder what becomes of the child's innate curiosity, their thirst for knowledge, and their longing to explore the world with unabashed wonder. What happens when their spirit is confined, their questions silenced, and their sense of self-worth diminished? The consequences may manifest in various ways, from acts of bullying and self-harm to the tragic incidents of violence that haunt our society.

It is imperative to recognize that the child's inherent nature is not one of "badness" but rather one of authenticity, curiosity, and the capacity for growth. The path towards a more harmonious existence lies in embracing and nurturing these innate qualities, allowing the child to unfold naturally and flourish in an environment that celebrates their unique essence.

It is indeed a distressing scenario to witness the repeated mantra of "be good" permeating a child's life, echoing in their ears from all directions. The weight of this message, like a venomous arrow, pierces deep into the core of their being, striking at the very foundations of their self-worth and self-confidence. It is a precarious territory, one that has the potential to shape and mold their adult selves if not approached with utmost care and sensitivity. Yet, there seems to be little time for such considerations.

The ringing of the bell signals a disruptive interruption, abruptly cutting off the child's emerging interests and curiosities. It redirects their attention to the next subject, leaving them with a sense of unfulfilled exploration. It is as if they were just beginning to uncover something meaningful, a thread of understanding that had captured their curiosity. But alas, the interruption disrupts the flow of thought and disrupts the natural rhythm of their learning journey.

In the midst of this relentless demand to "be good," children gradually internalize the belief that they must conceal their true selves. They learn to hide their authentic nature, convinced that they are inherently flawed or "bad," and that their survival and acceptance depend on projecting a facade of goodness. It becomes a survival mechanism, a coping strategy to navigate a world that seems to demand conformity and stifles individuality.

This process of self-concealment leaves a profound impact on their sense of identity and their ability to express themselves authentically. It breeds a dissonance between their true inner selves and the persona they present to the world. The tension between the two can be a source of great inner turmoil and confusion, shaping their interactions and relationships as they navigate through life.

It is crucial for us to recognize the significance of this struggle and the potential long-term consequences it carries. By acknowledging and addressing the harmful effects of the constant pressure to "be good," we can create spaces and environments that foster authenticity, acceptance, and genuine self-expression. Only then can children reclaim their innate worth and embrace the freedom to explore and grow without the constraints of judgment and pretense.

"I loathed every day and regret every moment I spent in a school."
—Woody Allen

Children, like Pavlov's dogs, become conditioned to conform to societal expectations in order to receive the rewards of acceptance, praise, gold stars, and love. However, it is essential to note that the love bestowed upon them is often conditional, contingent upon their ability to "be good." This conditional love is a stark departure from the concept of unconditional love, as it imposes a requirement that children meet certain expectations before they are deemed deserving of love.

Such a conditioning process does not align with the natural course of human development as shaped by evolution, nature, and instinct. Instead, it represents a man-made construct, a confining cage in which individuals are coerced to lead lives akin to those of slaves, trained dogs, or experimental monkeys. Its ugliness is profound, yet it is a reality that many prefer to turn away from, unwilling to confront the unsettling notion that everything they once believed to be true may be built on falsehoods.

It is crucial for parents to ask themselves a fundamental question: "Do I want my child to truly learn and grow, or do I simply desire for them to be trained to appear as though they are learning?" It is essential to recognize that children are in a perpetual state of learning, absorbing knowledge like sponges, regardless of the specific activities they engage in.

However, within the confines of the school system, children are instructed to abandon their intrinsic desires and interests, as they are deemed insignificant or worthless. They are dictated to by the authorities: "This is what is important. Pay attention and be good." The educational system force-feeds them a predetermined curriculum, disregarding the child's natural inclination to explore and discover in fields such as science, physics, or technology.

It is disheartening to observe that today's teachers have limited autonomy in shaping the educational experience. In contrast to decades past, where exceptional teachers could make a difference, today's educators find themselves administering tests and adhering to the common core curriculum—a standardized set of government-mandated standards that overlook individual differences and treat all children as if they were uniform entities.

In this era of educational conformity, the rich tapestry of diverse interests, talents, and potentialities that children possess is often overlooked or suppressed. The one-size-fits-all approach stifles their innate curiosity and hampers their ability to explore their unique paths of learning and growth. It is a system that fails to nurture the individuality and distinctiveness of each child, instead favoring a homogeneous and standardized approach.

As the bell rings, calling us back to the confines of the school, it becomes evident that the current education system perpetuates a constrained and restrictive environment. The challenge lies in recognizing the limitations of this system and striving to create alternative educational models that celebrate the diverse capabilities and potentialities of every child, fostering an environment where genuine learning, creativity, and self-expression can flourish.

Indeed, Mr. Anthony Esolen eloquently captures the essence of the educational system and its effects on children in his book "*Life Under Compulsion: Ten Ways to Destroy Humanity in Your Child.*" He astutely points out that the presence of the bell in schools symbolizes the utilitarian purpose that permeates all aspects of education. The bell's arbitrary command signifies that nothing is of ultimate concern, as everything is subject to its determined schedule.

Esolen raises the question of why we study things that do not hold ultimate significance or bring us the profound delight that love and beauty offer. The answer, he suggests, lies in utilitarian justifications or the lack of choice. Education becomes a means to an end, a tool of dubious quality. This perspective reduces education to a mere instrument rather than an experience that nourishes and enriches the human soul.

In our society, children are often treated as tools, labeled as "our greatest resource" or mere pawns in a socio-political game. They are not valued for their intrinsic worth but rather for what they can achieve. Their education is oriented towards molding them to fit into the Teaching Machine, which judges them based on arbitrary standards that have implications for their future in college and employment. Esolen masterfully critiques this mindset, highlighting the paradoxical nature of the system's laxness in teaching while imposing severe judgments that shape a child's trajectory.

Esolen's insights challenge the notion that there exists a universally applicable body of knowledge that every individual must possess.

The Common Core State Standards Initiative, for example, aims to establish a standardized set of learning goals for all students, emphasizing college, career, and life readiness. However, this one-size-fits-all approach disregards the diverse paths and interests that individuals may pursue in their lives.

Children are constantly told to "pay attention," a phrase that undermines their natural inclination to explore, learn, and be curious. It is disheartening to witness the stifling effect this constant implication has on children's innate desire to engage with the world around them. One may even speculate on the potential link between this narrative and the prevalence of attention deficit labels, but delving into that topic requires a separate conversation.

Esolen's thought-provoking book sheds light on the inherent flaws of the education system and calls for a reevaluation of its purpose. It invites us to consider the true value of education, not as a mechanistic tool, but as a means to cultivate the inherent humanity and potential of each individual child.

"One had to cram all this stuff into one's mind, whether one liked it or not. This

*coercion had such a deterring effect that, after
I had passed the final examination, I found the
consideration of any scientific problems
distasteful to me for an entire year."*
–Albert Einstein

In the confines of traditional schooling, the
rigidity of the alphabet becomes strikingly
apparent. The limited interpretation that "A" is
for apple permeates the educational system,
leaving little room for alternative perspectives.
It is a singular truth enforced upon the
students, an unquestionable decree that
suppresses individuality and divergent
thinking.

The prescribed notion of "A" is for apple is
ingrained in the structure of the curriculum,
perpetuating the idea that there is only one
correct answer. Other possibilities and
interpretations are undermined, deemed
worthless or disruptive. The child who dares to
suggest that "A" could represent something
different, perhaps an angel or an adventure, is
met with reprimand and judgment. The child's
desire for acceptance, appreciation, and the
freedom to express their unique self is silenced
under the weight of conformity.

The education system molds students to fit within the predefined boundaries of knowledge, leaving little room for personal exploration and creative thinking. The focus is on obtaining the correct answer, earning gold stars and passing grades, rather than fostering a genuine understanding of the world and encouraging individuality.

It is no wonder that alternative associations, such as envisioning the teacher in Pink Floyd's 'The Wall' who punished students with ruler-wrapped knuckles, come to mind. Such imagery symbolizes the restrictive and oppressive nature of an education system that enforces a narrow worldview and stifles the authentic voices of its students.

However, it is essential to note that this perspective is not about promoting disrespect or defiance, but rather about questioning the limitations imposed by the education system and advocating for a more expansive and inclusive approach to learning. The desire to embrace different interpretations of "A" or any other aspect of education reflects the innate human need for freedom of thought, individuality, and self-expression.

In conclusion, the confinement of "A" to solely represent an apple in the educational context highlights the systemic limitations and the suppression of diverse perspectives. The call to recognize and value alternative associations is not an act of rebellion but a plea for a more inclusive and enriching educational experience that celebrates the multifaceted nature of human existence.

Indeed, the question of whether the educational establishment truly nurtures critical thinking and independent thought or simply produces individuals who can regurgitate the "correct answer" is a profound one. It raises concerns about the nature and purpose of education itself.

Paul Goodman, a keen observer of the educational landscape, aptly remarked that the present motives of schools do not align with teaching authentic literacy. Reading, as a means of liberation and cultivation, is not fostered through a simplistic approach like "Run, Spot, Run." This highlights the limitations of a system that fails to inspire true curiosity and intellectual growth.

Beneath the surface issues of reading and writing lies a deeper problem of "illearnacy," which refers to the acquired suppression of learning courage and initiative. Guy Claxton, in his work 'Wise Up,' emphasizes the need for a transformation in the educational paradigm to encourage these qualities in learners.

However, the reality for a child in school remains a monotonous repetition of the "A" is for apple brainwashing. Day after day, week after week, the child is immersed in a system that reinforces a limited perspective and discourages independent exploration. The weight of authority figures, including parents, teachers, and society as a whole, perpetuates the notion that the child's natural inclination to explore and learn autonomously is insignificant and inconsequential.

The prevailing belief is that if it is not taught by these authoritative sources, it does not constitute genuine learning. This narrative undermines the innate human capacity for continuous learning and growth. Learning is not confined to the walls of a classroom or the directives of an education system; it is an inherent part of human existence, constantly evolving and expanding throughout life.

Therefore, the idea that children must attend school solely to learn is a fallacy. Children are natural learners, and their capacity for acquiring knowledge is ever-present. It is not an optional feature but an integral component of their being.

In conclusion, the reiteration of the "A" is for apple indoctrination is a stark reality for children in the education system. It raises fundamental questions about the purpose of education and the stifling of innate curiosity and independent learning. As we contemplate the implications of these concerns, it becomes evident that education should be a catalyst for fostering lifelong learning, empowerment, and the fulfillment of each individual's innate potential.

"I am beginning to suspect all elaborate and special systems of education. They seem to me to be built up on the supposition that every child is a kind of idiot who must be taught to think."
–Anne Sullivan

It is true that many individuals, caught up in the demands of work and school, may not be aware that there is an alternative path, a different way of approaching family life and personal fulfillment. They may still be influenced by outdated ideologies and parenting advice, such as that of Dr. Spock. However, it is important to note that there are contemporary resources available, such as the work of Dr. Sears, which offer a more humanistic and holistic approach to parenting.

In seeking answers and solutions, we sometimes overlook the simplicity of the message or the power of a single quote, sign, or story. "*Grasper: A Young Crabs Discovery*" by Paul Owen Lewis is a children's book that conveys a profound lesson. It tells the story of a crab who ventures beyond the familiar confines of its tide pool, discovering new possibilities and courageously returning to share its message with the other crabs who remained behind.

This concept of stepping outside one's comfort zone and embracing individual thought is intriguing. It invites us to consider the potential for personal growth and transformation when we are willing to explore new perspectives and challenge established norms. "Grasper" offers a valuable lesson for both children and adults alike.

While some may find themselves trapped in old programming and societal expectations, it is essential to seek out alternative resources and perspectives that align with our values and aspirations. By embracing new ideas and encouraging individual thought, we can navigate a path of personal fulfillment and create a more meaningful and harmonious family life.

Human Survival

When examining the history of the family and its transformation, we encounter various perspectives and insights. Professor Ruth Wisse of Harvard emphasizes the impact of the Women's Liberation movement on the American home, likening its effect to that of communism on the Russian economy.

"Women's Liberation, if not the most extreme, then certainly the most influential neo-Marxist movement in America, has done to the American home what communism did to the Russian economy, and most of the ruin is irreversible. By defining between men and women in terms of power and competition instead of reciprocity and co-operation, the movement tore apart the most basic and fragile contract in human society, the unit

from which all other social institutions draw their strength. "

By shifting the focus from reciprocity and cooperation to power and competition between men and women, the movement disrupted the fundamental and delicate contract that underpins human society—the family. This development has had far-reaching and, in many cases, irreversible consequences.

Author Erin Pizzey further underscores the significance of family life as the foundation of any civilization.

"Family life was and always will be the foundation of any civilization. Destroy the family and you destroy the country."

She asserts that the destruction of the family equates to the destruction of the country itself. While these statements encapsulate complex issues, they underscore the crucial role played by the family in society.

The unraveling of the family unit can be traced back to the industrial revolution, when mothers began leaving their homes to work and entrusted the care of their children to impersonal institutions such as daycare. Throughout history, the family unit had been considered essential for human survival. However, as society changed, the fabric of the family was deconstructed and eroded.

Additionally, J.H. Van der Berg provides insights into the gradual disintegration of family ties and shared activities.

"Children go to school from the time they are four or five years old. By the time they leave school forever, they are no longer able to be educated, in the original meaning of the word. The sick are not nursed at home; even the chronically sick are removed from their families more and more frequently. The old people disappear into homes for the aged more often than in the past. This disappearance is felt to be necessary by both young and old: life changes so quickly and fundamentally that one cannot expect old people to adapt themselves continuously to the ways of their children. Clothes are made at home less and less often. Food is not stored for the winter. Remedies are no longer prepared at home. Even recreation is sought elsewhere. Families who still give parties at home are becoming scarce. The custom of group

singing, accompanied by the harmonica, violin, or guitar played by one of the family or a neighbor has died out - replaced by the relentless noise of a cackling or jingling contraption, recently brought to perfection by the addition of a screen, which has definitely put an end to all activity."

He highlights how various aspects of life, including the care of the sick and elderly, clothing production, food storage, and recreational pursuits, have shifted away from the home and family domain. This disconnection from traditional family practices has only been exacerbated by the prevalence of modern technologies and digital media, which consume much of our attention and time.

Imagining life without the conveniences of modern technology and media is indeed challenging. The pervasive presence of electronic devices, online worlds, and video games has greatly altered the dynamics of family life and the ways in which children learn by example. Reflecting on the prospect of living as families did over a century ago, with minimal reliance on electricity and media, prompts us to consider the potential benefits of reconnecting with simpler, more intimate ways of living.

In essence, exploring the historical changes in the family unit and contemplating a life disconnected from modern technology invites us to question the impact of these developments on our well-being, relationships, and the transmission of knowledge from one generation to the next. It encourages us to reevaluate the values and practices we hold dear and consider how we can cultivate a more balanced and fulfilling family life in the context of our rapidly evolving world.

Storytime Exercise

I challenge you to embark on a transformative journey, one that transcends the confines of reality and delves into the realm of imagination. Together, let us venture to the verdant park, where nature's sublime beauty envelops us, and the ethereal melodies of birdsong serenade our souls. With the literary masterpiece "*Sarah, Plain and Tall*" by the esteemed Patricia MacLachlan firmly grasped in our hands, we relinquish the distractions that encumber our minds and embark on a voyage of literary exploration.

As we delve into the pages of this captivating novel, we are transported to the late 19th century, a bygone era imbued with rugged charm and untamed frontiers. Here, in the heartland of the western United States, we encounter Jacob Witting, a widowed farmer burdened by the weight of sorrow and the daunting task of single-handedly managing his farm and raising his two children, Anna and Caleb. Plagued by the lingering anguish of his departed wife, Jacob seeks solace in the prospect of companionship, prompting him to place an audacious advertisement for a mail-order bride.

Enter Sarah, a courageous woman hailing from the coastal landscape of Maine. Drawn by the allure of a new beginning and fueled by her own unspoken yearnings, she embarks on a transformative journey across vast distances to answer Jacob's call. Through their tender courtship and the emergence of an unconventional family unit, we bear witness to the resilience of the human spirit and the indomitable power of love.

Now, you may wonder how this poignant tale relates to the sphere of schooling and education. Allow me to illuminate the connection. In our collective quest for knowledge and enlightenment, books and movies hold tremendous potential to shape our understanding of the world and awaken our innate curiosity. They serve as vessels for storytelling, weaving narratives that resonate with our deepest emotions and resonate within the chambers of our hearts. Through the artful tapestry of words, we find ourselves transported to different times, places, and perspectives, expanding our horizons and nourishing our souls.

In an era dominated by digital distractions and fragmented attention spans, the profound significance of literature cannot be overstated. It serves as a beacon of wisdom, transmitting timeless lessons and virtues that transcend the boundaries of time and space. While many modern creations may serve as mere entertainment, there are still treasures to be discovered, narratives that capture the essence of our shared humanity and offer profound insights into the human condition.

As we sit amidst the tranquility of the park, the rustling of leaves harmonizing with the turning of pages, let us embrace the transformative power of storytelling. Let us celebrate the enduring beauty of family, the resilience of the human spirit, and the boundless potential of education to ignite our imaginations and kindle the flames of enlightenment. Through the synergy of literature and the natural world, we embark on a profound journey of self-discovery and collective understanding.

With each word read and every emotion evoked, we honor the timeless tradition of oral storytelling, rekindling the flame of our ancestral heritage. While the village storyteller may have been replaced by electronic devices, the essence of their craft endures within the written word. It is through literature, through the medium of books and films, that we continue to learn, grow, and deepen our connection to the world around us.

As the sun casts its golden hue upon the horizon, illuminating the park in a final burst of radiant light, we emerge from our literary sojourn with hearts full of gratitude. Gratitude for the profound wisdom captured within the pages of "Sarah, Plain and Tall," gratitude for the transformative power of storytelling, and gratitude for the enduring legacy of education to shape our lives.

In the embrace of nature's tranquility, we realize that the lessons we learn through literature extend far beyond the boundaries of the classroom. They offer us insight into the complexities of human relationships, the resilience of the human spirit, and the profound impact of love and acceptance. Through the art of storytelling, we gain a deeper understanding of our own experiences and the world around us.

As we close the final chapter of "*Sarah, Plain and Tall,*" our hearts are touched by the transformative power of family bonds and the triumph of the human spirit over adversity. We are reminded that education is not confined to the walls of a classroom or the memorization of facts. It is a lifelong journey of exploration and self-discovery, fueled by the wisdom imparted through literature and the stories we encounter along the way.

Let us carry the lessons of "*Sarah, Plain and Tall*" with us as we continue our own personal and academic odysseys. May we strive to embrace the values of compassion, resilience, and the courage to forge our own paths. And may we, in turn, become storytellers ourselves, weaving narratives that inspire, uplift, and ignite the flame of curiosity in future generations.

As we bid farewell to the park, our minds and hearts enriched by the profound experience of literature, let us venture forth with renewed purpose and a deep appreciation for the power of storytelling. For in the pages of books and the enchantment of film, we find the keys to unlocking our imaginations, expanding our understanding, and nurturing our souls. The journey continues, and with each story we encounter, we grow closer to becoming the best versions of ourselves.

So, my friend, I extend my gratitude for this shared journey of exploration and enlightenment. May we continue to embrace the transformative power of literature, cherishing the timeless wisdom and beauty that it imparts. And let us remember, in this ever-changing world, the enduring value of family, the significance of education, and the magic that lies within the stories we tell.

As we part ways, may your own path be illuminated by the light of knowledge and the joy of storytelling. Until we meet again on our next literary adventure, may you find inspiration, solace, and growth in the stories that shape our lives.

Farewell, and may your journey be filled with wonder and discovery...

Indeed, the *Sarah* series and the "*Little House on the Prairie*" series evoke a profound sense of longing for a way of life that may feel distant and unfamiliar in today's world. Through the captivating narratives and vivid portrayals of these stories, we are transported to a time when family and community were integral to daily existence.

As we immerse ourselves in the lives of the characters, we are reminded of the importance of interdependence and the deep connections forged through shared experiences. The values of resilience, self-sufficiency, and the unyielding spirit of pioneers resonate within us, inspiring a yearning for a simpler, more connected way of life.

It is natural for our children, growing up in a fast-paced and technologically driven society, to feel a sense of longing and nostalgia for the communal bonds and self-sufficiency depicted in these stories. The contrast between the modern lifestyle and the agrarian settings portrayed in the series is stark, and it heightens our appreciation for the enduring values of family, community, and self-reliance.

As we watch these series and reflect on the vanishing way of life they depict, we are compelled to seek out glimpses of that world in our own lives. Whether it be through travels to distant lands or creating intentional communities, we yearn for a sense of connectedness and shared purpose that seems elusive in our fast-paced, individualistic society.

The power of these stories lies not only in their ability to transport us to a bygone era but also in their capacity to ignite within us a desire for a more meaningful and authentic existence. They serve as reminders that amidst the modern conveniences and distractions, there is a longing for a deeper connection to our roots, to our families, and to the natural world.

So, as we indulge in the nostalgia and yearning awakened by these stories, let us also strive to infuse our present lives with the values and lessons they impart. Let us cultivate a sense of community, foster resilience, and embrace the importance of family and interconnectedness.

In this journey of reflection and longing, may we find solace in the stories that touch our hearts, and may they inspire us to create a world where the values of family, community, and self-reliance are cherished and celebrated once again.

J.H. van der Berg's poignant reflections from "*The Changing Nature of Man*" resonate deeply with the longing for a sense of community and connection that seems to have been lost in the modern world. His recollections of the vibrant conversations and interactions among neighbors in the backyard evoke a sense of nostalgia for a time when differences of opinion were embraced as opportunities for understanding and growth.

In those days, quarrels were not seen as fractures in relationships but rather as moments of engagement and dialogue. The shared space of the backyard fostered a common atmosphere that transcended individual differences, allowing for lively discussions that reverberated against the walls and brought people together. The act of quarreling was a sign of mutual understanding, and the aftermath of such disputes often became woven into the fabric of the community, symbolized by the hen houses, rabbit crates, and other communal structures.

During leisurely summer evenings, neighbors gathered on steps and chairs, engaging in conversation, storytelling, and even singing. The children, quietly listening, absorbed the richness of these interactions until they were gently sent off to bed. This collective presence created a tangible sense of togetherness, a real and vibrant group that existed beyond mere proximity.

In those times, neighbors were more than strangers living next door; they were familiar faces who extended a helping hand during times of illness or need. The saying that "a near neighbor is better than a distant cousin" held true, as the bonds of community were strong and reliable. However, with the passing of time, the neighbor has transformed into a stranger, and the distant cousin, now equipped with a car, has become a more accessible figure. Yet, this accessibility is fleeting, as everyone is consumed by their own busyness and distance has replaced connection.

The loss of these communal activities and meaningful interactions leaves us with a void—a missing piece in the tapestry of our humanity. Neil Postman's warnings in *"Amusing Ourselves to Death"* resonate deeply in today's context, where individuals retreat into their own handheld devices, distancing themselves from the shared experiences of the present moment. Even mothers, in their attempt to ensure the safety and well-being of their children, resort to monitors instead of nurturing the vital human contact that fosters connection and bonding.

The consequences of this widening gap and disconnection are profound. Loneliness seeps in, and a sense of exile pervades our lives. We yearn for the return of those rich and meaningful interactions, for the weaving together of our collective experiences that make us truly human.

Reflecting on van der Berg's poignant observations, let us recognize the importance of reclaiming and preserving the essence of community, of engaging in conversations that bridge the gaps between us. Let us create spaces and moments where we can come together, where the distance is minimized, and the power of human connection is rekindled. In doing so, we can heal the loneliness, mend the fractures, and find solace in the shared experience of being truly present with one another.

In the landscape of the present day, our handheld devices have become ubiquitous companions, constantly at our fingertips. They have created a new paradigm of interaction where physical proximity is no longer a guarantee of shared presence. Consequently, we find ourselves increasingly isolated, fragmented, and distanced from one another.

Mothers, too, have adapted to this digital era, resorting to monitors to keep a watchful eye on their babies. While driven by the genuine desire to ensure their child's safety, these monitors inadvertently create a barrier, separating mother and child from the raw and intimate human contact that is essential for nurturing bonds and fostering emotional connection.

This increasing reliance on digital devices perpetuates a widening gap—a chasm that grows between us and those around us. The physical proximity that once naturally facilitated communal interaction is now overshadowed by a prevailing sense of disconnect. Loneliness, a persistent companion in our modern lives, finds fertile ground in these fragmented relationships. It is a profound exile from the warmth and richness of genuine human connection.

Amidst the ceaseless hum of technology and the constant lure of digital distractions, we must pause and reflect upon the consequences of this increasing distance. What are we sacrificing in the pursuit of constant connectivity? What are the costs of trading genuine, present interactions for virtual facsimiles?

To bridge this widening gap, we must consciously seek opportunities to reestablish human contact. We must create spaces and moments where devices are set aside, and the focus shifts back to the people around us. It is through genuine face-to-face conversations, shared experiences, and intentional presence that we can reclaim our sense of belonging and rebuild the connections that have frayed.

Children as Exiles

The introduction of J.H. van den Berg and his seminal work, *"The Changing Nature of Man"*, invites us to delve deeper into the profound transformations that have shaped the relationships between adults and children throughout history. Van den Berg, a Dutch psychiatrist and researcher in phenomenological psychotherapy and metabletics, dedicated his scholarship to understanding the evolving nature of human existence within specific historical and social-cultural contexts.

Central to van den Berg's exploration was the notion of "metabletic sense," denoting significant shifts in human phenomena that heralded new ways of life and meaning across various realms of human activity. His inquiry encompassed the intricate web of relationships between men, women, and children in their dynamic interplay with one another, with the material world, and with the spiritual realm.

In his illuminating work, van den Berg draws attention to the profound separateness of the child's world, urging us to witness the distinctiveness of their experiences. To fully grasp this separateness, he suggests observing a playground, shedding the lenses that romanticize every interaction as an act of love. What becomes apparent is a fenced-in space, an island of relative safety amidst the overwhelming maturity of the adult world—an island of necessary exile.

Van den Berg elucidates the protective mechanisms put in place when children venture onto the streets, where they must be armed against the dangers that lie ahead. Crossing guards guide them, halting the traffic to ensure their safe passage. In this moment, the children form a group of exiles, momentarily shielded from the perils of a world not yet meant for them. This act of protection, while seemingly benevolent, stems from a profound acknowledgment of the irreparable harm inflicted upon them.

His work beckons us to reflect on a time when the boundaries between adult and child were less defined, when a different understanding of childhood prevailed. The profound shift that has occurred since then raises questions about progress and its implications. Van den Berg's insights challenge us to critically examine the consequences of these transformations and contemplate whether they have truly propelled us in a positive direction.

As you engage with van den Berg's thought-provoking ideas, ponder the implications of this historical journey. Consider the ways in which our perception of children has changed over time and the profound implications it holds for the present and future. Van den Berg's work serves as a catalyst for introspection and an opportunity to reevaluate the paths we have traversed in our pursuit of progress.

Van den Berg highlights the diminishing visibility of modern maturity, emphasizing how children in the past could witness various trades being practiced in accessible locations. The rope-maker, the smith, the brazier, the cooper, the carpenter—all carried out their work in places where children could observe and imagine themselves participating in those trades in the future.

However, in the present era, many trades have become confined to factories, spaces that children are not allowed to enter. This separation prevents children from gaining a true understanding of what transpires within these closed-off realms. Moreover, the emergence of professions that are not easily discernible to children adds another layer of invisibility. How can a child comprehend their father's work as a superintendent, a social worker, a tax collector, or a psychotherapist? The actual nature of these occupations eludes the child's grasp, leading to a sense of emptiness and meaninglessness associated with them.

Van den Berg admits to his own profession as a psychotherapist and acknowledges that his children's lack of interest in pursuing the same path brings him relief. He reflects on how his work is largely hidden from his children's view, as they only witness patients visiting his office and the subsequent silence that ensues. Similarly, the son of a factory worker faces the barrier of closed doors, unable to accompany his father to the workplace or gain insight into his daily activities. This separation denies children the opportunity to witness their fathers' labor and be immersed in their experiences.

The consequence of this lack of visibility is the gradual disappearance of a time when children had some sense of choice regarding their future occupations. Previous generations could recall a time when they had at least some knowledge of the potential paths available to them. However, with the passing of these generations, the memories of an uncertain time of choice built on limited visibilities will fade. Institutions, purportedly addressing an age-old deficiency, now prescribe occupations, depriving individuals of the freedom to make choices based on what lies ahead rather than on what is currently visible.

Van den Berg predicts that future choices will be constrained to what appears most probable or least impossible from an inventory of pre-existing options. The act of making a choice will be preceded by an inventory, a cataloging of predetermined possibilities. The delay in making this inventory stems from the desire for justifications that could legitimize the choices being made. The innate invitation and anticipation inherent in making a choice will gradually erode, replaced by the practicality of selecting from preordained alternatives.

In the face of these shifts, van den Berg's profound observations compel us to reflect on the consequences of diminishing visibility and restricted choices. We are prompted to consider the impact on children's understanding of their future paths and the potential loss of anticipation and invitation that once animated the act of making choices. The exploration of van den Berg's work invites us to critically examine the implications of these societal changes and to reconsider the essence of true choice and autonomy in the modern world.

Van den Berg continues his exploration of the diminishing concept of choice in our modern era, where the future appears empty and the individual making the choice feels equally empty. He highlights the shifting dynamics of decision-making, emphasizing that soon the act of choosing will be reduced to selecting what seems most probable or least impossible from a predetermined inventory. This process of making an inventory will be delayed for as long as possible, as the search for something that might justify a choice becomes increasingly elusive.

In the past, the factors influencing choice were external to the individual. They resided in the future, not within the person making the decision. The elements that guided choices were found outside of oneself, providing a sense of direction and anticipation. However, in our present time, these elements are expected to reside within the individual. Yet, as van den Berg points out, no one enters life with a pre-determined program or a clear path. The emptiness of the future is mirrored by the emptiness within the individual.

Consequently, individuals are encouraged to postpone making choices, waiting for some form of external validation or justification. This delay is evident in the expert's advice to a mother, suggesting that her child is still too immature and should first go through college before making decisions. However, even after completing higher education, many individuals still find themselves unsure of their path. The expert then attributes this uncertainty to a deficiency in the available inventory of options or the immaturity of the individual. The solution proposed is often to extend the period of education or seek further qualifications, perpetuating the postponement of choice.

This perpetual deferral of choice reflects the prevailing emptiness and lack of clarity in our society. The individual is left waiting, searching for something that may never materialize. The expert's insistence on prolonged education and the continuous quest for external validation contribute to the sense of emptiness within individuals, perpetuating a cycle of indecision.

Through his analysis, van den Berg prompts us to critically examine the consequences of delaying choice and relying on external validation. He challenges us to question the notion of readiness and maturity, raising concerns about the impact on individuals who are constantly pushed to defer decision-making in the absence of a clear path. Ultimately, his words invite us to reflect on the nature of choice itself and the importance of fostering a genuine sense of purpose and direction in our lives.

Knowledge that is acquired under compulsion obtains no hold on the mind."

–Plato

Van den Berg's essay, written in 1961, delves into the historical transformation of childhood and the family structure in Western society. He highlights how, for centuries, children were regarded as miniature adults who actively participated in and understood the adult world. However, as the 18th century unfolded, life for both adults and children became increasingly complex, divided, and inaccessible. Children gradually emerged as distinct beings with their own unique ways of being, thinking, and feeling.

During the latter part of the 18th century, not only did childhood as a concept emerge, but the modern family also took shape, distinct from the traditional family structures of the past. The accelerated pace of societal change in the 20th century further exacerbated the complexity and divisiveness of society, placing children in a vulnerable position and making it increasingly challenging for them to navigate their way to maturity and active participation in adult life.

The establishment of schools became the solution to this societal shift, with the intention of "raising children right." However, it is noteworthy that for the preceding centuries, such institutionalized constructs did not exist. Children were separated from their families, removed from natural environments, and segregated from adults under the belief that schools were necessary for their education. Van den Berg astutely observed the profound changes and unsettling nature of Western society after World War II, characterized by disorder and instability. He recognized the need to understand and consider the influence of social and cultural factors on people's behavior, relationships, and overall mental well-being during this era of societal upheaval.

Over fifty years have passed since van den Berg penned his essay, and society has continued to evolve. The magnitude of change has only intensified, pushing us further away from the historical context he explored. It is a testament to the ongoing shifts and challenges faced by individuals and families in an ever-changing world.

"Don't pay attention to other people's minds. Look straight ahead, where nature is leading you – nature in general, through the things that happen to you; and your own nature, through your own actions."

–Marcus Aurelius

How We Learn

Returning to the subject of learning, we encounter the wisdom of Albert Einstein, a prominent figure of our time. He asserted,

"I never teach my pupils; I only attempt to provide the conditions in which they can learn."

This viewpoint prompts us to question the innate nature of learning and its juxtaposition with the artifice of teaching.

By examining what we commonly refer to as "primitive" societies, we observe the absence of formal schools and structured instruction. Nevertheless, these communities exhibit remarkable harmony and success. Bertrand Russell astutely remarked,

"Men are born ignorant, not stupid; they are made stupid by education."

In such societies, knowledge transmission occurs organically, with the young learning from their elders, the older children learning from adults, and occasionally even the adults learning from the children. Mutual respect and a sense of awe accompany the sharing of wisdom by the elders, who have accumulated the most extensive life experience.

Curiously, there is no designated authority responsible for teaching in these communities. Instead, individuals within the village pursue learning autonomously and continuously, embodying a profound power. The absence of pressure regarding what is learned or missed stems from a collective understanding that each individual will acquire precisely what they require. This natural process of learning resists augmentation and defies attempts to impose external structures, as our endeavors to do so have proved unsuccessful.

Why, then, are our educational institutions, in which we confine children on a daily basis, unable to enhance learning beyond the child's intrinsic motivation? The answer lies in the very nature of learning itself, for children are in a perpetual state of learning. It is imperative to emphasize this point: children are learning at all times. While it is true that children acquire knowledge within the confines of school, we must consider the true essence of what they are learning.

Is the child learning to conform, to suppress their voice and diminish their sense of worth? Are they internalizing the notion that their time is inconsequential, that their ideas and creations hold little value? Are they being conditioned to believe that adhering to a particular behavior is the key to acceptance and success? Perhaps they are even acquiring negative behaviors such as cheating or exerting aggression upon those who are vulnerable and weaker.

The rigidity inherent within the school environment itself inadvertently impedes a child's intellectual growth, hindering rather than nurturing it. The restrictive nature of this system suppresses the child's natural drive for learning and their innate human instincts. These instincts, inherent from birth, form the additional components accompanying our human existence.

To truly grasp the essence of learning, we must acknowledge that it surpasses the mere acquisition of vast quantities of information. Education, in its most profound sense, should strive to awaken and cultivate a child's natural capabilities, rather than seeking to indoctrinate and constrain through traditional notions of teaching. The challenge lies in understanding and embracing the multifaceted nature of learning and recognizing that the most potent educational experiences arise from the inherent curiosity, creativity, and passion that reside within each child.

If one truly seeks to unravel the fallacies of compulsory education, then Paul Goodman's book "*Compulsory Miseducation*" is an essential read. Goodman fearlessly exposes the school system as another institution that convinces individuals of their dependence on its services. Written in the 1960s, this thought-provoking work serves as a poignant reminder that human beings are inherently free and possess the capacity to shape their own lives outside the confines of institutionalized schooling.

It is crucial to recognize that children are not only born free, but they also possess an innate drive and instinct for learning. As a homeschooling and unschooling parent, my role as a teacher was simply to foster a love of learning, a task that proved relatively easy given their inherent disposition. The ability to learn independently empowers children to continue acquiring knowledge throughout their lives, adapting to new needs, interests, and goals as they emerge.

My primary responsibility was to step aside and create an environment that catered to their individual learning styles and provided the necessary resources and tools they requested. As John Holt eloquently stated, "If children are given access to enough of the world, they will see clearly enough what things are truly important to themselves and to others, and they will make for themselves a better path into that world than anyone else could make for them."

The key to success in this endeavor lies in genuinely embracing the spirit of adventure and exploration with one's child. This entails venturing beyond the confines of home, visiting libraries, engaging with various events and activities that stimulate curiosity and provide valuable information. Merely indulging in passive activities like watching soap operas all day at home does not reflect a genuine interest in adventure and exploration. It requires venturing out into the world, asking questions, and actively engaging with the diverse opportunities for learning that surround us.

Unschooling is indeed not a "hands-off" approach where parents simply walk away from their children's education. As a parent of an unschooled child, one assumes certain responsibilities to facilitate and guide the learning process. This includes providing resources, support, guidance, information, and advice to help children access, navigate, and make sense of the world around them.

For instance, parents can share interesting books, articles, and activities with their children, introducing them to new ideas and avenues of exploration. They can also assist in connecting their children with knowledgeable individuals who can further enrich their interests. These individuals can range from physics professors to automotive mechanics, offering valuable insights and experiences. Additionally, parents can help their children set goals and guide them in figuring out the steps necessary to achieve those goals.

Teaching children to question everything is a fundamental aspect of unschooling. Parents should encourage their children to ask questions about everything, even if they already know the answers. By modeling curiosity and engaging in questioning, parents empower their children to think critically and develop their own investigative skills. This approach can begin from a young age, as even toddlers exhibit a natural inclination to ask "why" and seek understanding.

Engaging in conversation and asking "why" to individuals encountered in everyday life can be a rich source of learning. Whether it's the postman, the grocery clerk, or the vegetable vendor at the farmer's market, initiating conversations and seeking knowledge from those around us can provide valuable insights. People are often delighted to share their expertise and engage in meaningful conversations, as humans are inherently social creatures. By making connections with various individuals, children can expand their understanding of the world and see everyone as potential teachers.

Unschooling involves active participation from parents in facilitating their children's learning. By providing resources, guidance, and encouraging curiosity through questioning, parents can create an environment that fosters exploration and continuous learning. Embracing the social nature of human interaction and seeking knowledge from diverse sources further enriches the unschooling experience.

Indeed, there may be skeptics who argue that people are busy or encounters with certain individuals may not always be positive. In response, I offer two suggestions. Firstly, exercise your freedom of choice and seek out alternatives if you find that a particular interaction or experience is unsatisfactory. Secondly, ask yourself how you can contribute to making someone else's experience a little better. In the context of your child's learning, have faith that they are capable of navigating their own educational journey.

It is not uncommon for parents to question themselves more than their children due to their own experiences in traditional schooling. However, it is important to trust your instincts and recognize that your child's learning at their own pace is a positive sign. As a parent, you have the ability to stretch your imagination and explore educational possibilities beyond the confines of a public-school education.

It is crucial to remind ourselves that nature and our evolution follow natural processes, whereas school is a man-made construct—an idea conceived by someone. While it may have had good intentions initially, it has since become distorted, damaging, and far removed from meeting the needs of children. The original intent of sending children to school was to provide them with opportunities for a better life. Paradoxically, it seems that today, opting out of school presents an even greater opportunity for a better life.

School, as it exists today, is not what we set out to build. It has transformed into an institution that can resemble a factory or even a prison. Its rigid structures and standardized approach often stifle individuality and hinder the natural learning processes that children possess. By recognizing these limitations and seeking alternatives, parents can break free from the confines of the institutionalized schooling system and embrace a more holistic approach to education.

Immersion

Human instinct drives us to survive and strive for success. However, the concept of success varies from person to person. It can encompass financial and material achievements, but it can also encompass happiness and a sense of well-being. What if true success lies in the freedom to pursue one's passions and desires?

In the context of education, we should shift our focus from knowledge being imposed upon the child to the child actively pursuing knowledge. As George Bernard Shaw eloquently stated.

"We want to see the child in pursuit of knowledge, not knowledge in pursuit of the child."

As parents, the crucial question we should ask ourselves is whether we are providing our children with the necessary tools to navigate the challenges of this rapidly changing world. One effective approach I have discovered is immersion in the subject at hand. This immersion can take various forms, ranging from a week-long intensive study to a month or even a year of deep engagement.

Even in the case of very young children, immersion may mean a few hours of focused exploration. However, to truly master a subject, one must fully immerse themselves in it. By providing opportunities for immersive learning experiences, we can empower our children to develop a deep understanding and proficiency in their chosen pursuits.

I share favorite Chinese proverb:

Tell me and I will forget
Show me and I may remember
Involve me and I will understand

Indeed, the power of hands-on, immersive learning is truly remarkable. When we engage in activities that we are passionate about, whether it's a hobby, pastime, or sport, we naturally become deeply involved and retain a wealth of knowledge and understanding.

Consider your own favorite activity or interest. For instance, if you're an avid stamp collector, you likely possess a vast amount of knowledge about stamps that sets you apart from the majority of people. Others would perceive you as an expert or master in the field simply because of your passion and accumulated knowledge. This didn't happen because someone forced you to study stamps for a specific duration of time. Instead, you chose to pursue stamp collecting, and as you delved into the subject, gathering information on prized, unique, or rare stamps, you naturally retained the facts because they were relevant and valuable to your stamp collecting endeavors.

The essence of human passion lies not merely in the realms of theoretical knowledge but in the experiential depths of personal immersion. Such is the case with our neighbors, each fervently engaged in their chosen hobbies, poised as experts within their respective domains. Within the tapestry of our community, one finds an ardent collector, fervently acquiring comics and Elvis memorabilia, illuminating a world hitherto unseen by those who lack the same zealous dedication. His intimate familiarity with the minute details, the nuances of editions, artists, and narrative arcs, showcases the mastery he has cultivated through unwavering commitment.

Conversely, residing across the street resides a knitter, a soul whose passion for the craft extends far beyond the mere creation of textile wonders. For hours on end, she regales us with tales of yarn weights, material origins, and the enthralling history woven within the fabric of textiles. Her knowledge, an intricate tapestry itself, unfurls with each passing conversation, illustrating her profound understanding of the subject matter. And in the same enclave of domesticity, her spouse, a devout sports enthusiast, possesses an encyclopedic wealth of scores, plays, and anecdotes dating as far back as the fabled year of 1950. His memory retains the names and numbers of players, coaches, and the triumphs and tribulations that have punctuated the annals of athletic pursuits. As he passionately lectures his wife, absorbed in her knitting, one cannot help but ponder the extent to which her interest may wane in the face of such statistical intricacies.

Is it conceivable that she would harbor recollections of long-forgotten scores from the bygone era of 1960? The likelihood seems faint, for her heart's devotion lies in the realm of yarns and their manifold textures, not in the annals of athletic triumphs. Similarly, does her partner, the sports enthusiast, possess an understanding of the delicate variances between mohair, wool, alpaca, and other fibers? To query whether he possesses such knowledge or even nurtures an affinity for it is to tread upon uncharted terrain.

Within the realm of our intertwined lives, these neighboring souls exhibit the beautiful asymmetry of human passion. They venture forth, driven by their innate curiosities, embracing the worlds that align with their individual interests. Each domain boasts its own language, its unique tapestry of knowledge, meticulously woven through the threads of fascination and personal resonance. It is within this tapestry that we witness the harmony and dissonance of our human pursuits, an ever-present reminder that our deepest passions stem from the resolute pursuit of what we find meaningful and relevant.

Thus, as we reflect upon these neighbors and their divergent paths of knowledge, we are reminded of the intricate tapestry that constitutes human experience. We are beckoned to celebrate the idiosyncrasies that render each of us a custodian of our passions, forever weaving our own narratives and retaining the knowledge that shapes our personal realms of interest.

Now, as we delve deeper into the intricacies of the educational paradigm, we are faced with a glaring incongruity that escapes the grasp of logic. While it may not require the intellect of a prodigy or the prowess of a rocket scientist to comprehend, the essence of our argument resonates with most rational minds. We find ourselves in a perplexing scenario where children are expected to remain seated and absorb fragmented sound bites of information throughout the entirety of their formative years, seemingly as though it were an interminable lifetime.

These young minds are deprived of the tactile sensations, the olfactory delights, the visceral experiences that bring knowledge to life. They possess no genuine relationship with the information thrust upon them, no inherent connection to its essence. Yet, we audaciously demand that they retain this standardized knowledge, disregarding their diverse developmental stages, their disparate socioeconomic backgrounds, and their unique ways of perceiving and engaging with the world. We remain apathetic to their challenges and the lives they lead beyond the confines of the classroom, oblivious to their physical transformations as they navigate the tumultuous realm of growth. We accept as the norm that they must simply endure the rigors of schooling.

"Why must they go to school?" we ask. The response, all too familiar, echoes through the corridors of authority: "Because I say so. Because it is expected. Because it is the way things are." The fundamental absurdity of this unnatural mode of learning, the inherent contradictions, and deficiencies, eludes our collective consciousness.

Yet, millions of children are subjected to this daily ordeal. Coercion breeds no love for any pursuit. Compliance fails to awaken their innate capabilities or unearth their hidden talents; instead, it fuels a simmering cauldron of resentment. At this juncture, I must draw your attention to an enlightening tome by Dr. David R. Hawkins MD PhD, titled "*Power Versus Force: The Hidden Determinants of Human Behavior.*" Within its pages, the author unveils a compelling dichotomy – force, an incomplete entity reliant on external energy, juxtaposed against power, a force that stands alone in its totality, requiring no external dependencies or demands.

Force consumes, siphoning life and vitality, while power invigorates and breathes life into existence. Power emanates from compassion and self-affirmation, whereas force is mired in judgment and engenders feelings of inadequacy. Learning, at its core, is an embodiment of power, a force that propels individuals to new heights of understanding and self-realization. Schooling, on the other hand, manifests as force, a constraining and limiting framework that stifles the boundless potential of young minds.

Homeschooling or Unschooling

I am intrigued by the concept of lifelong learning and the continuous exploration of knowledge. It fascinates me to witness the curiosity and growth in both myself and others. As for my child, I am dedicated to understanding their interests and passions, regularly checking in with them to foster open communication and sharing.

When I became a parent, I had a profound realization that I needed to become the best version of myself because my child was watching and learning from my example. This realization ignited a deep desire to embody qualities such as unconditional love, forgiveness, patience, mindfulness, and presence. While I initially felt I was doing this for my child, it turned out to be a transformative gift for myself as well.

The journey of parenthood has been a catalyst for my personal growth and spiritual development, an ongoing path that continues to unfold. Through this experience, I have discovered a profound sense of wealth and satisfaction that goes beyond material possessions. As parents, we have the responsibility to educate ourselves, seek guidance and mentorship, stay informed, nurture our own growth, and provide support for one another.

This reciprocal process of learning together strengthens the bond between parent and child, fostering trust and mutual respect. It builds confidence, self-esteem, and a deep sense of worth for both parties. It creates a sense of belonging and a recognition of being part of something greater than oneself, laying the foundation for compassion, patience, and understanding. Furthermore, it equips us with the skills to perceive obstacles and challenges as opportunities for further learning, growth, and expansion.

"You learn at your best when you have something you care about and can get pleasure in being engaged in."
–Howard Gardner

Homeschooling and unschooling are two approaches to education that offer alternatives to traditional schooling.

Carol Ann Tomlinson, author of *'The Differentiated Classroom'* wrote:

"It is not so important to have all the answers as to be hungry for them."

In homeschooling, parents take on the responsibility of making educational decisions for their child, determining how best to provide education. On the other hand, unschooling empowers the child to make decisions about their own learning. It means allowing children to learn what they want, when they want, and in the way they want, driven by their own motivations.

In unschooling, the learner has control and choice, while seeking outside help from parents, mentors, books, or formal lessons as needed. The emphasis is on the child taking ownership of their education and making decisions about their learning journey. Unschooling operates on the belief that children are just as clever and capable as adults, and they have the innate ability to direct their own learning.

John Holt, in his book *"Teach Your Own"*, challenges the notion of the home as a better school, emphasizing that its value lies in the fact that it is not a school at all. The home becomes a supportive environment for children to grow and learn in their own unique ways, unrestricted by the structures and limitations of traditional schooling.

When children are allowed to design their own learning path, incredible alternatives emerge. They showcase their brilliance and potential when given the opportunity to explore and express their unique interests and talents. This is where hackschooling comes into the picture, and we can listen to voices like Logan LaPlant to gain insight into this approach:

"I'm not tied to one particular curriculum, and I'm not dedicated to one particular approach. I hack my education. I take advantage of opportunities in my community and through a network of my friends and family. I take advantage of opportunities to experience what I'm learning, and I'm not afraid to look for shortcuts or hacks to get a better, faster result.

It's like a remix or a mashup of learning. And here's the cool part: because it's a mindset, not a system, hackschooling can be used by anyone, even traditional schools."

Logan LaPlant, a 13-year-old speaker and advocate, coined the term "hackschooling" to describe a mindset and approach to education that challenges and transforms existing systems to work differently and better. He believes that hackers are not limited to computer geeks, but rather individuals who think innovatively and are willing to question and change established systems.

For Logan, hacking is not limited to technology; it extends to various aspects of life, including skiing and education. He sees hacking as a mindset that can change the world. He cites notable figures like Steve Jobs, Mark Zuckerberg, and Shane McConkey as examples of individuals with the hacker mindset who have made significant impacts in their respective fields.

At the heart of Logan's perspective is the idea that education should prioritize not only academic knowledge but also the pursuit of happiness and well-being. He questions why schools often separate the pursuit of happiness and health from education, suggesting that they should be integrated into the educational experience. Logan sees happiness and health as essential practices that should be given equal importance alongside traditional academic subjects.

Logan's viewpoint challenges the conventional boundaries of education and highlights the need to rethink the purpose and scope of schooling. His ideas invite us to consider the holistic development of individuals, emphasizing not just intellectual growth but also their overall well-being.

Logan LaPlant acknowledges the influence of Sir Ken Robinson's renowned TED talk on "*How Schools Kill Creativity*," emphasizing the importance of creativity in education. He believes that creativity should be given equal importance to literacy and treated with the same status. In his concept of hackschooling, Logan highlights three key components: being healthy, happy, and creative, all while adopting a hacker mindset.

Recognizing the changing cultural and technological landscape, Logan calls for schools to evolve and adapt to better meet the needs of today's children. He urges parents to consider alternative approaches to education, even if they believe their circumstances might not initially allow for it. One suggestion is to form co-ops or collaborative learning groups where parents can share the responsibility of teaching and create smaller "classes" based on shared interests.

The underlying message is that the mind, like a parachute, can only work when it is open. This book serves as an invitation to open one's mind, explore different educational possibilities, and find ways to prioritize the holistic development and individual needs of children in today's rapidly changing world.

In my personal belief, the loss of trust in our own essential nature has contributed to a general mistrust of children and human nature itself. This mistrust is often rooted in unmet needs during infancy and childhood, where a lack of recognition and validation can lead to a disconnection from our inherent qualities of confidence, joy, and love. As a result, society becomes characterized by unpleasantness, danger, unhappiness, alienation, and instability, as we conform to societal expectations rather than embracing our true nature.

Our beliefs shape our experiences, and our beliefs are largely influenced by what we have been taught by our parents, schools, and mainstream culture. However, it is crucial to consider the possibility that what we have been told may be flawed or incomplete. By bravely awakening to this truth, we can question the system we have blindly followed and start trusting ourselves and our children once more. This entails creating the time and space to put this trust into practice, allowing our natural instincts and innate wisdom to guide our decisions and actions.

What if we made a deliberate choice to grant our children the freedom to navigate their own path? What if we allowed them to shine and thrive, just like Logan LaPlant's parents did for him? Let's take this concept even further and extend it beyond the boundaries of school, encompassing every aspect of their lives, twenty-four hours a day.

Imagine if I were to propose that we never do anything for our children that they can do for themselves, even if it may take a little longer. I understand that it may test our patience, as we are often in a rush. But what if this is an opportunity for us to pause, to learn the value of patience, and to simply wait?

Will the world really crumble if we take a step back and allow our children to take ownership of their own actions? Is the world more important than our child, or is our child the world?

Give your child the message from the very beginning that you expect him to figure things out for himself.

Perhaps you haven't considered that when we opt for quick fixes and rush to do things for our children, we inadvertently send them the message that they are incapable or inefficient. Moreover, we deny them the chance to learn in that moment and hinder their faith in their own abilities to accomplish and problem-solve.

Instead, what if we take a few extra minutes here and there, allowing our children the space to figure things out on their own? These moments of independent exploration and problem-solving are true quality time, far more meaningful than superficial play dates on Sunday afternoons.

The ultimate goal is to cultivate trust in the process and gradually rebuild mutual trust and respect, not only between parent and child but within the entire family unit. This approach not only enhances the educational journey but also nurtures stronger family bonds.

Imparting the message from the very beginning that we expect our children to figure things out for themselves fosters self-reliance and independence. It cultivates a sense of security within them, regardless of the circumstances surrounding them.

"What makes people smart, curious, alert, observant, competent, confident, resourceful, persistent - in the broadest and best sense, intelligent- is not having access to more and more learning places, resources, and specialists, but being able in their lives to do a wide variety of interesting things that matter, things that challenge their ingenuity, skill, and judgment, and that make an obvious difference in their lives and the lives of people around them."

–John Holt

In my personal experience, I refrained from doing things for my children not because I was a neglectful parent, but because I recognized the potential harm in interfering with their natural process of learning and growth. By stepping out of their way, I allowed them to navigate their own paths. I encourage you to do the same.

"We come to experience a profound unconditional love not by finding the perfection in a child, but by seeing them perfectly as they are."

–Kytka

I discovered that empowering my children to trust their own nature was unnecessary because the inclination to trust is inherent within us from birth. As parents, we simply need to give ourselves permission to step back and allow it to unfold naturally. We need to allow our children to simply be.

In our attempts to fill our children with everything, we inadvertently strip away much of what they are born with. Let us put an end to this cycle of damage and abuse. It's time to let go of the old ways and acknowledge that we were doing our best with the information we had at the time.

Indeed, making the decision to let go of the need for constant measurement and comparison is crucial. Just as we don't measure and compare every step a child takes in their physical development; it is absurd to subject their learning journey to such scrutiny. Each child is a unique and original being, deserving of acceptance and celebration.

Understanding the truth of human nature and our innate drive to survive and thrive is paramount. When we embrace this belief, the universe will affirm it in countless ways. As evidence of the changing tides, even the architect of the "No Child Left Behind" initiative has publicly acknowledged its shortcomings and the detrimental impact of standardized testing on students, teachers, and schools.

Diane Ravitch, an educational historian, emphasizes the need for a generation of thoughtful thinkers who can reflect and engage with the world, rather than mere memorizers striving for passing grades. We must shift our focus from competing in the world to living and thriving in it.

"The child is curious. He wants to make sense out of things, find out how things work, gain competence and control over himself and his environment, and do what he can see other people doing. He is open, perceptive, and experimental. He does not merely observe the world around him, He does not shut himself off from the strange, complicated world around him, but tastes it, touches it, hefts it, bends it, breaks it. To find out how reality works, he works on it. He is bold. He is not afraid of making mistakes. And he is patient. He can tolerate an extraordinary amount of uncertainty, confusion, ignorance, and suspense ... School is not a place that gives much time, or opportunity, or reward, for this kind of thinking and learning."

The words of John Holt, penned over five decades ago, resonate powerfully. He eloquently describes the natural curiosity and eagerness to make sense of the world that children possess. They are open, perceptive, experimental, and unafraid of making mistakes. However, traditional schooling often fails to provide the time, opportunity, and encouragement for this kind of deep thinking and learning.

Revisiting Holt's wisdom allows us to fully appreciate its significance. His insights, shared before the current crisis in education, hold even greater value today. We would do well to heed his advice and create spaces that honor and nurture children's innate curiosity, boldness, patience, and thirst for understanding.

Now, armed with new knowledge, we can make informed decisions that better serve our children and allow us to grow alongside them. It is important to forgive ourselves and release any blame or resentment we may hold towards others. We must stop holding onto such negativity that no longer serves us.

Learning Journey

Embarking on my own personal journey, I have wholeheartedly embraced the art of questioning alongside my children. This practice, instilled from their tender years, continues to resonate within me even as they have transitioned into adulthood.

"It is among the commonplaces of education that we often first cut off the living room and then try to replace its natural functions by artificial means. Thus, we suppress the child's curiosity and then when he lacks a natural interest in learning he is offered special coaching for his scholastic difficulties."

–Alice Duer Miller

Why indeed do we subject our children to an environment that fails to align with their innate learning patterns? Is it due to our own preoccupations, our busyness that blinds us to their needs? Or perhaps, even more disconcerting, have we lost the capacity to contemplate deeply and reflect upon what is truly in their best interest? Have we become oblivious to our own cognitive faculties?

The individual mind, akin to a computer terminal connected to a vast database, possesses the potential to tap into the collective consciousness of humanity. This database, the repository of human consciousness itself, encompasses the realm of genius. Every human, through the mere act of existence, possesses access to this wellspring of wisdom.

It is an immense privilege for me to bear witness to the remarkable and awe-inspiring journeys my children embark upon. Take, for instance, my son, who has authored several books, including "*Immersion Mastery*." This accomplishment was not something I expected or imposed upon him. It arose from a deep inner calling within him, and I hold it in reverence. When he was merely 10 years old, he had already written a book titled "*My Journey to Becoming a Mayan Shaman*," documenting his experiences in pursuit of his passion to become a shaman. I supported and encouraged him on this path of self-discovery.

Now, he is driven by a fervent desire to share his lived experiences and insights. He witnesses the plight of broken children, desperate for help and seeking solace amidst the chaos that surrounds them. They gravitate towards him, seeking guidance in making sense of the madness that engulfs their lives. He extends his compassionate hand, offering alternative perspectives and pathways. Their gratitude is palpable.

He has assumed the role of mentor and coach, rescuing these young souls from the precipice of despair. He has steered them away from the treacherous paths of substance abuse and even averted tragic consequences such as suicide. The cries of these children in crisis go unheard in our society, yet he has become a beacon of hope for them, lending his ear and wisdom to their pleas for understanding.

We must acknowledge that the voices of these struggling children deserve to be heard.

In the profound words of John Holt, true leaders are not those who merely amass a following but rather individuals who forge their own path with unwavering conviction, regardless of whether anyone chooses to accompany them. Leadership qualities encompass traits such as courage, endurance, patience, humor, adaptability, resourcefulness, tenacity, a pragmatic outlook, and the ability to maintain composure even in the face of adversity. These qualities do not mold individuals into followers, but rather empower them to become leaders in their own right.

Holt's insights, as conveyed in his influential work "*Teach Your Own*," have significantly shaped my perspective on nurturing the educational journeys of my children. I have embraced an approach that allows learning to gracefully intertwine with the rhythm of their lives. Learning is an intimate and personal endeavor, akin to the very essence of their souls and existence.

I hold steadfast in my commitment to preserve their autonomy, refraining from imposing my own worldview or past experiences upon them. Even in the most subtle ways, I am mindful of not encroaching upon their unique and individual experiences. Their exploration, discovery, challenges, joys, and engagement with the world are theirs to embrace fully.

As a parent, my role is not to dictate their paths or superimpose my vision onto their lives. Rather, I strive to create an environment that nurtures their innate curiosity and fosters their inherent potential. I celebrate their journey of self-discovery and empower them to shape their own understanding of the world. In doing so, I honor their individuality and grant them the freedom to cultivate their own perspectives, insights, and wisdom.

The dance of learning unfolds delicately and harmoniously within their lives, guided by their own inner compass. I am humbled to witness the beauty and richness that emerges from this authentic, self-directed exploration. Their learning journeys become a manifestation of their true selves, each step paving the way for growth, fulfillment, and the realization of their own unique purpose.

In essence, my approach embodies the spirit of Holt's teachings, wherein I embrace the role of a facilitator, a guide, and a nurturer, allowing my children to become leaders in their own right.

Allow me to share a fascinating anecdote that may raise some eyebrows, particularly those of my dear mother (apologies, Mom!). You see, my mother has a peculiar habit of vocalizing her eating experiences, offering remarks such as "Mmmmm, this is so sweet" or "Oh, I cannot eat this, this is disgusting" or "Why do you eat that, it isn't sweet at all," and so forth. While this may seem innocuous, it holds a deeper significance.

Years ago, as my mother expressed her thoughts about food in this manner, I noticed my son, Zack, casting a questioning gaze at his own plate. At the time, I paid little attention to this unfolding dynamic, unsure whether it was a conscious process or worthy of deeper contemplation.

However, a few days or weeks later, as we sat at the table once more, Zack uttered a surprising statement: "I am not eating this, Mama, it is disgusting." Startled, I looked up from my own plate, as I knew this particular dish was one of his absolute favorites. Puzzled, I responded, "Really? I recall you telling me that you liked it."

Zack's reply held a revelation: "I know, Mama, I did. But that was before Babi told me it was disgusting." (Babi, meaning "grandma" in Czech, refers to my mother.) This incident exemplifies how children are incessant learners, absorbing knowledge and perceptions from their surroundings. In this case, what did Zack learn?

It is worth noting that my mother did not overtly lecture him on the disgusting nature of the dish, nor did she clandestinely manipulate his thoughts through hypnotic means. Yet, he internalized her remark and allowed it to shape his perspective. It is a perfect illustration of how children continuously learn, even in the most subtle ways.

Of course, I took it upon myself to have a late-night phone conversation with my mother, delivering a lecture on the importance of acknowledging that each individual possesses unique taste buds and preferences. I emphasized that my children should be allowed to develop their own culinary experiences and that her unintentional influence could distort their perception of food. It was a stern conversation, perhaps even extreme, but as a protective mama bear, it was my duty to be vigilant and ensure my children's learning experiences were beneficial rather than detrimental.

Looking back, I can now chuckle at the intensity of that interaction. Yet, upon reflecting on the underlying principles I explained, the gravity of the situation becomes apparent. My son's sense of taste was being inadvertently influenced by someone with a distinct biological makeup, chemistry, and personal preferences. How unfair it was for his own sensory experience to be distorted in such a manner.

As a parent, I embrace the power and responsibility of nurturing my children's voices and experiences. It is within the sanctuary of our home that I can wield this influence. However, the dynamics change drastically in the realm of formal schooling, where such control is entirely beyond my reach.

Thus, my role as a parent extends far beyond mere laughter or stern conversations. It demands heightened vigilance, an unwavering awareness, and a protective stance. It is my duty to ensure that my children absorb knowledge and experiences that will ultimately benefit them, shielding them from potential harm. This sacred responsibility lies within the realms of my home, where I have the privilege of safeguarding their growth and well-being.

So, while I can now find amusement in the extreme measures taken during that conversation, it serves as a poignant reminder of the profound influence that even the subtlest interactions can wield over a child's development.

Going to Bat for Your Child

This is where the essence of learning truly takes root, and it is essential that we remain conscious and aware of this process. We must create an environment that fosters optimal learning experiences by providing the right surroundings and support.

Moreover, it exemplifies what I refer to as "going to bat for your child," an unwavering commitment to fiercely protect them from potentially damaging influences. I didn't realize it then, but I was engaged in an arduous journey of personal growth and development. I was dedicated and committed, engaging in a form of Olympic-like training to become the best version of myself as a mother. And yet, in a matter of moments, my mother's words could undo all my efforts. Such a situation was simply unacceptable. If she wished to be a guest in our lives, she needed to be conscious of and respectful towards my parenting choices.

Setting boundaries became imperative. As a parent, it is our responsibility to establish clear boundaries, to stand strong in our convictions. There are no excuses, no slacking off. It is an inherent part of the parental role that we signed up for the moment we brought our child into this world. We must always advocate for our children, being their voice when necessary. And it is crucial that they witness this advocacy, carried out with kindness and gentleness. In doing so, they learn that we genuinely want what is best for them, which ultimately allows them to make their own choices. The side effect of this approach is that it builds trust between parent and child. What a powerful dynamic to cultivate - trust and respect.

When you establish this trust with your child, both of you embark on a journey of growth, learning, and expansion. This principle extends beyond homeschooling or unschooling; it applies to every child. All children are constantly influenced by their surroundings and the people they encounter.

As your mindset shifts and you awaken to the profound journey of parenting, you begin to observe your environment and the people around you more closely. Your awareness becomes acute, and you become a conscious and awakened parent. Thoughts arise, such as questioning the suitability of Chuck-e-Cheese as a birthday party venue. You start to delve deeper, considering the values and meaning behind a birthday celebration. How do you want your child to experience the significance of their birth? Is it through materialistic possessions and excessive stimulation, or can it be something more meaningful?

Your awareness becomes a guiding force, and your intuition begins to serve you. You develop a sense of inner knowing that directs your choices. In our family, for instance, we choose to share gifts in the form of heartfelt poems and letters, expressing our deepest feelings and appreciation for one another. Believe it or not, this is more than enough. In fact, these heartfelt expressions become cherished treasures within our family.

By embracing this perspective, we create an environment where genuine learning flourishes, and our children grow with a deep sense of trust, respect, and love.

I find solace and liberation in not succumbing to the pressures of societal norms that urge me to keep up with the materialistic desires of the world. My children are not burdened with the need to possess the latest gadgets or conform to societal expectations. They do not seek validation through material possessions, nor do they feel the need to fit in based on external acquisitions. In fact, the allure of the latest and greatest gadgets holds no sway over them. Their wish lists, if they had any, would likely be devoid of such gadgets.

Instead, my focus lies in providing them with books, tools, and resources that nourish their minds and enrich their learning journey. We often find these treasures in the library or through the close-knit community of friends we have cultivated. Through sharing and trading, we foster a culture of collaboration and resourcefulness. It is in this way that I honor their true essence, their authentic presence, and their individual beings each and every day. And in return, they honor me in the same manner. We exist as a family bound by love and respect, but we are also the closest of friends. We genuinely enjoy one another's company and cherish the time we spend together.

I find it perplexing that modern culture and society perpetuate the notion that this kind of familial bond and friendship is impossible to achieve, especially during the teenage years. Contrary to these preconceived notions, my experience has shown me otherwise. My children and I have cultivated a deep and meaningful connection that transcends stereotypes. We navigate the teenage years with understanding, empathy, and open communication. The idea that teenagers are inherently difficult or resentful towards their parents is far from my reality.

In truth, it is not so difficult to foster such a loving and harmonious environment. It requires a shift in mindset, a commitment to prioritize genuine connection, and an unwavering belief in the power of love and respect. By defying societal expectations, we have discovered a profound bond that strengthens us and brings immeasurable joy to our lives.

Kids to the Back

Let us delve deeper into the realm of schooling and its implications in a rapidly changing world. We must critically examine what transpires when children are separated from the broader world and confined within the confines of their peer group. Does this preparation truly equip them for the complexities of real life?

Consider this: Do adults spend their entire lives primarily interacting with a group of individuals who are all the same age? Isolation within a homogenous age group does not reflect the realities of the world awaiting these children. Outside the school walls lie a diverse tapestry of individuals from various backgrounds, circumstances, and age groups. Are children being taught how to relate and interact with people of all ages in school? From my observations, the focus seems to be more on fostering pack mentality and succumbing to peer pressure rather than nurturing genuine social skills.

In fact, let us temporarily set aside our personal beliefs and embedded values and view the matter from a purely logical perspective. Could we perhaps argue that schools, with their practice of segregating children based on ability, achievement levels, and age, are, in essence, perpetuating a form of segregation? This notion poses a profound question regarding a child's civil rights. After all, if Ms. Rosa Parks no longer needs to sit at the back of the bus, why should our children be confined within the walls of a school?

The reality of schooling involves the systematic segregation of students based on various criteria. Children are classified as "gifted" or "slow learners," and their community within school consists primarily of same-age peers. Parents often have limited knowledge or influence over their child's peer group. While proponents of conventional schooling argue that children need school to become socialized, the actual social environment within schools can be far from healthy. Factors such as age segregation, a low ratio of adults to children, limited contact with the broader community, a lack of exposure to individuals in various professions beyond teachers and school administrators, the emphasis on high-achieving students, the shaming of struggling students, and the prevalent emphasis on passive sitting all contribute to an artificial construct of reality and hinder the child's social development.

In this artificial construct, children are pulled away from the familiarity of home and subjected to a rigid structure dictated by bells and schedules. The value and worthiness of this experience are rarely questioned; instead, the expectation is that children simply must comply and attend school.

It is crucial to ask ourselves if children truly perceive the value in this educational system. Are they being empowered to navigate the world with confidence and adaptability? Or are they merely enduring a system that fails to meet their individual needs and stifles their natural curiosity and love for learning?

It is time for us to critically evaluate the impact of traditional schooling and explore alternative approaches that prioritize the holistic development and individualized growth of each child. Only by challenging the status quo and embracing new possibilities can we create an educational landscape that truly serves the needs of our children in an ever-evolving world.

Indeed, the contrast between unschooling and traditional schooling becomes even more pronounced when we consider the social development of unschooled children. By having the freedom to engage with their greater community, unschooled children have the opportunity to form connections with individuals of various ages and backgrounds. This enables them to relate to a wider range of people and find their place within more diverse groups, fostering a more holistic understanding of society.

Critics of unschooling often argue that removing a child from the "ready-made peer group" found in traditional schools hampers social development. However, numerous studies consistently demonstrate that unschooled children tend to display greater maturity compared to their schooled counterparts. This maturity is a direct result of the diverse range of people with whom unschooled children have the chance to interact on a daily basis.

When we consider the long-term implications, which approach serves children better in life? Is it the rigid confines of traditional schooling or the freedom of unschooling that allows them to explore their interests and develop a deep understanding of the world around them? It is worth reflecting upon.

In this modern age of rapidly advancing technology and evolving societal structures, we must question our role in imposing outdated ideas, systems, and processes upon our children. Shouldn't our children have the right to pursue their own interests and engage in the ever-changing landscape of knowledge and skills? By embracing alternative educational approaches like unschooling, we can empower our children to adapt, learn, and thrive in a world that is constantly evolving, without confining them to outdated models of education.

It is essential that we, as parents and educators, reconsider our approach to education and ensure that we are providing our children with the tools and opportunities to become lifelong learners, critical thinkers, and adaptable individuals in an ever-changing world.

It is an intriguing proposition to consider allowing students to test their teachers and to have a more active role in shaping the educational experience. Such an approach would shift the traditional power dynamics and promote a more collaborative and student-centered learning environment. While it may initially sound unconventional or even radical, it prompts us to question the existing system and explore alternative possibilities.

Critics may argue that such ideas are impractical or unrealistic, but it is important to remember that education should be a dynamic and evolving process that adapts to the needs and interests of learners. By allowing students to have a greater say in their education, we foster a sense of ownership and engagement, leading to deeper learning experiences.

Furthermore, when we examine the history and purpose of public education, we may uncover underlying motivations that go beyond purely educational objectives. The book "*The Underground History of American Education*" provides a comprehensive exploration of this topic, shedding light on the control and indoctrination aspects of the public school system. It presents a perspective that challenges the mainstream narrative and invites readers to critically examine the foundations of our educational institutions.

"Education is a weapon, whose effect depends on who holds it in his hands and at whom it is aimed."

–Joseph Stalin

Research also suggests that students who are not confined to the traditional schooling system tend to exhibit higher levels of intelligence, self-reliance, analytical thinking, and independence. This is attributed to their continuous and experiential learning, unrestricted by the boundaries of a classroom. By embracing the idea that the entire world can serve as a classroom, we open up endless possibilities for meaningful learning experiences.

While these concepts may seem unconventional or even radical, they prompt us to question the status quo and reimagine education in ways that better serve the needs and potential of learners. By embracing a broader view of learning and challenging the existing structures, we can create educational environments that truly empower and inspire our children.

Unschooling embraces the belief that children are naturally curious and have an innate desire to learn. It recognizes that learning can take place in various contexts and through diverse experiences, including play, household responsibilities, personal interests, internships, travel, books, elective classes, family interactions, mentors, and social engagement. By allowing children to pursue their own interests and take the lead in their learning, unschooling aims to make education more meaningful, relevant, and useful to the individual child.

One of the fundamental criticisms of traditional schooling is that it often follows a rigid, standardized curriculum that treats all students as if they have the same needs, interests, and learning styles. Unschooling challenges this approach, suggesting that it is inefficient to force children to learn specific subjects in a predetermined manner, pace, and timeline, without considering their unique circumstances and individuality. By providing a more personalized and flexible learning environment, unschooling seeks to enable children to explore subjects that truly resonate with them and to learn at their own pace and in their own way.

It is important to note that unschooling distinguishes between education and learning. Education is often associated with formal schooling, while learning is viewed as a lifelong process that occurs in various settings and through a multitude of experiences. Unschooling advocates argue that traditional schools, with their standardized curriculum and structured routines, may not align with the natural ways in which individuals acquire knowledge and skills. Instead, they advocate for a more organic and individualized approach to education that recognizes and nurtures children's innate curiosity and desire to learn.

Ultimately, unschooling challenges the notion that school is the sole or primary source of education and argues for a more holistic and flexible approach to learning that acknowledges and values the diverse pathways through which individuals acquire knowledge and grow.

"We ask children to do for most of the day what few adults are able to do for even an hour. How many of us, attending, say, a lecture that doesn't interest us, can keep our minds from wandering? Hardly any."

–John Holt

In the poignant words penned by John Holt in his illuminating work, "How Children Fail," we are confronted with a profound reflection on the formidable task we impose upon young minds within the confines of a conventional educational institution. Holt astutely observes that even as adults, we struggle to maintain our focus and intellectual engagement during a lecture that fails to pique our interest. Such a predicament compels us to pause and question the unquestioned assumption that schools are the sole domain of learning for our children.

Therefore, I beseech parents, in their noble pursuit of the best education for their progeny, to embark upon a journey of self-education and enlightenment. Take it upon yourselves to conduct thorough research and diligent study. Inquire incessantly, seeking answers to the perennial "why" that reverberates within the depths of our curiosity. For in this pursuit of knowledge, we unearth a reservoir of understanding that transcends the boundaries of convention and tradition.

In this quest for enlightenment, let us not overlook the profound query: Who, indeed, is the guiding hand that shapes and molds the tender minds of our beloved offspring? Within the realm of traditional schooling, the child's teacher is assigned by the school's administration, their expertise designated by grade level or subject matter. However, in the realm of alternative educational paradigms such as homeschooling or unschooling, the mantle of the educator is often donned by the parent themselves. This noble responsibility grants them the liberty to fashion a personalized and malleable approach to pedagogy, one that harmonizes with their child's unique inclinations and aspirations.

Let not the veil of complacency descend upon our discerning minds. Rather, let us, as vigilant stewards of our children's education, undertake a journey of intellectual exploration, questioning the status quo. Embrace the charge to unveil the mysteries of education, for therein lies the path to enlightenment and empowerment for our beloved progeny.

From Classrooms to Crime

Parents of school children often find themselves with limited influence over the selection of their child's instructors and teachers. However, in the realm of unschooling, a path that deviates from conventional educational norms, parents play a more pivotal role in the choice of coaches and mentors who guide their child's educational journey. This involvement fosters the cultivation of enduring and profound relationships, as parents become intimately acquainted with those who shape their child's intellectual and personal growth.

"I always like to learn, but I don't always like to be taught."

–Winston Churchill

It is crucial for parents to invest ample time in interacting with their child's teachers, moving beyond the confines of the customary parent-teacher conferences that often serve as mere glimpses into the educational landscape. In the corporate realm, these gatherings resemble orchestrated affairs, where appearances are meticulously curated to please higher-ranking individuals. Yet, in the context of our children's education, trust cannot be solely based on appearances. We must delve deeper, discerning the character and intentions of those entrusted with our children's learning. Our children, in their earnest trust, not only absorb the knowledge imparted but also internalize the traits, gestures, mannerisms, and even facets of the teachers' personalities.

Critics of unschooling perceive it as an extreme educational philosophy, expressing concerns about potential deficiencies in social skills, structure, and motivation when compared to their conventionally schooled peers. However, proponents of unschooling ardently argue the contrary, positing that self-directed education within a natural environment fosters a more resilient and adaptable child who is well-equipped to navigate the intricacies of the "real world."

Where, then, do we stand in this ongoing debate? Do we believe that children are incessantly learning, regardless of the educational setting? Do we harbor concerns about the identity of our child's teacher, the composition of their peer group, and the activities that occupy their school day? It is incumbent upon us, as parents, to recognize that every encounter and exposure molds the foundational emotions and beliefs that shape our child's sense of self.

The prevailing climate of security measures in schools today is undeniably disconcerting. Iron gates, imposing fences, and the presence of metal detectors create an atmosphere that feels distinctly incongruous with the realm of childhood. One cannot help but question the troubling image that emerges from this reality.

The presence of metal detectors, shootings, high fences, and lockdowns in schools is a distressing reflection of the current state of our society. It raises crucial questions about the underlying causes of this restlessness, aggression, and bullying. Are these measures of heightened security truly effective in addressing the root issues? It is doubtful.

The escalation of such security measures does not address the core problems that contribute to the breakdown of social harmony and the erosion of values. It is imperative to delve deeper into the underlying factors that lead to these societal challenges and seek meaningful solutions.

Consider the disconcerting notion of envisioning larger prisons instead of universities. While this may seem extreme, the reality is that the United States already incarcerates a staggering number of its citizens, both in absolute terms and as a percentage of the total population. The statistics are alarming, with the U.S. comprising only 5% of the global population but holding 25% of the world's prison population.

"But, good gracious, you've got to educate him first. You can't expect a boy to be vicious till he's been to a good school."
–H. H. Munro

Furthermore, there is a direct correlation between funding for prison construction and its impact on education. In California, for instance, the state witnessed the construction of 21 prisons and a 209% increase in prison funding from 1984 to 1994. In contrast, only one state university was built during the same period, with university funding seeing a mere 15% increase. These numbers shed light on the disheartening disparity between investments in correctional facilities and those in higher education.

Given the acknowledgment that the school system is broken, it is worth considering whether our entire society has become "schooled," as Ivan Illich suggests. Illich highlights that the traditional schooling system can foster a sense of dependency, affecting both the rich and the poor equally. This raises questions about what society is truly teaching and whether we even understand the essence of teaching itself.

It is crucial to critically examine our educational systems, the values they promote, and the skills they prioritize. By seeking a deeper understanding of teaching and learning, we can embark on a journey of transformation that addresses the root issues plaguing our society. Let us strive for an education that empowers individuals to think critically, nurture empathy and compassion, and cultivate a sense of social responsibility.

In this context, we must ponder whether our children have been reduced to mere commodities, stripped of their individuality and reduced to faceless names within the confines of an institutional system. It is within the walls of the school that such depersonalization seems most pronounced.

Therefore, I implore you once again to delve into the profound insights offered by books like *The Underground History of American Education*. Additionally, I urge you to explore the works of John Taylor Gatto, an esteemed educator with nearly three decades of experience in the classroom. His notable accolades, including being named New York City Teacher of the Year for three consecutive years and New York State Teacher of the Year in 1991, attest to the depth of his expertise.

In 1991, Gatto penned a powerful letter titled "I Quit, I Think," which he published in the op-ed pages of the Wall Street Journal. In this letter, he expressed his decision to retire from teaching, citing his refusal to continue "hurting kids to make a living." This courageous act marked the beginning of his influential career as a public speaker and writer, devoted to shedding light on the flaws of the education system. Gatto's invaluable contributions have been recognized through esteemed awards, including the Alexis de Tocqueville Award for Excellence in Advancement of Educational Freedom in 1997.

"These institutions that produce barely literate, dependent, conformist, incomplete individuals full of emotional and psychological problems, who lack real knowledge (and whose capacity for acquiring such is deliberately weakened or eliminated), and who are just educated' enough to pay their taxes and buy the latest products, are not, in fact, failing schools - on the con- trary, they are performing their designated function PERFECTLY. That purpose is to mold people in such a way as to make them more easily controlled by the corporations and the state."

– John Taylor Gatto

By dedicating time to explore the works of John Taylor Gatto and other insightful authors, you equip yourself with the necessary knowledge to make informed decisions about your child's education. Just as you readily invest hours in frivolous television programs or movies, I implore you to commit yourself to engaging with the material I recommend, for it pertains to the very life and future of your child.

"When someone considers himself to be totally governed by influences outside himself, he sits in apathy".

–Ruth Minshull

Let's take a moment to contemplate the essence of apathy, as expounded in the meticulous definitions we have perused. It elucidates a state characterized by an absence of emotional responsiveness and a dearth of interest in matters that typically evoke excitement, intrigue, or sentiment—a state of indifference.

In light of this analysis, let us direct our attention to the educational institution, aka, school. Does it not compel us to contemplate the presence of a substantial number of disengaged and apathetic students within our schools? Are these the very individuals who manifest tendencies towards bullying and inflicting terror upon their peers? Alas, the disheartening prevalence of child suicide and the alarming incidents of mass violence within school premises cannot be dismissed.

"The suicide rate among preteen and young teen girls spiked 76 percent, a disturbing sign that federal health officials say they can't fully explain. For all young people between ages 10 to 24, the suicide rate rose 8 percent from 2003 to 2004 - the biggest single-year bump in 15 years - in what one official called "a dramatic and huge increase."

–Associated Press

Indeed, it is with great sensitivity that we navigate this treacherous terrain, particularly for those who have entrusted the education of their children to these institutions. However, the pressing need for continued discourse compels us to confront these realities rather than retreat into an ostrich-like state of avoidance.

Thus, I implore you to proceed with open minds and unwavering resolve, for evading these pressing concerns shall not yield solutions. It is only through steadfast engagement and concerted efforts that we may aspire to comprehend the underlying factors perpetuating apathy within the educational sphere. By doing so, we inch closer to establishing a scholastic milieu that fosters genuine emotional connection, nurtures intellectual curiosity, and safeguards the well-being of our children. Let us embrace the gravity of this matter and work towards transformative change.

According to an insightful report from Healthy Place: America's Mental Health Channel, prevalent assumptions surrounding suicide attempts among children and adolescents warrant reconsideration. Contrary to popular belief, the primary motivations behind such tragic actions extend beyond mere manipulation, attention-seeking, or cries for help. When directly questioned following their suicide attempts, the responses provided by these young individuals parallel those of adults.

Remarkably, a significant proportion—approximately one-third—expressed a profound desire for death itself. Another one-third disclosed their aspiration to escape from seemingly insurmountable predicaments or distressing states of mind. Astonishingly, a mere 10% of respondents admitted to seeking attention through their actions. Those who genuinely yearned for death exhibited heightened levels of depression, anger, and perfectionism, indicative of their diminished self-esteem and self-worth.

In essence, these troubled young souls perceived themselves as inadequate and unable to meet societal expectations. The burden of their self-imposed standards proved overwhelming, driving them to contemplate the most devastating of measures: ending their lives. This heartbreaking reality underscores the urgency of fostering a compassionate environment that cultivates a sense of worth and belonging for every child, alleviating the crushing weight of self-judgment and unattainable standards.

"How could youths better learn to live than by at once trying the experiment of living?"
–Henry David Thoreau

Indeed, it is deeply disheartening to contemplate any circumstance or condition that could lead a child to experience such profound despair that they contemplate taking their own life. As human beings, our instinctual drive is to survive and flourish, to embrace life with all its challenges and joys. Therefore, the notion that a child would be subjected to such overwhelming pressures and emotional anguish begs for urgent reflection and action.

While various factors may contribute to a child's distress, it is crucial to acknowledge the significant roles played by the home environment and the educational system. These two spheres hold immense influence over a child's development, shaping their perceptions of themselves, their capabilities, and their worth. Consequently, it is essential to create nurturing environments that prioritize the well-being, emotional resilience, and holistic growth of children.

No child should ever be made to feel so burdened, so lacking in self-worth, or so engulfed by hopelessness that they contemplate ending their life. Our collective responsibility as a society is to foster environments that cultivate love, understanding, and support for every child. This requires a reevaluation of societal expectations, educational practices, and parenting approaches to ensure that children are empowered to embrace life with confidence, purpose, and the knowledge that their existence is valuable and cherished.

Seeking Answers

Indeed, the pursuit of knowledge and understanding is a fundamental aspect of human nature. We have been bestowed with an innate curiosity that drives us to seek answers, explore new perspectives, and grow intellectually. It is through this seeking that we uncover the truths and insights that shape our lives and the lives of those around us.

When it comes to the education of our children, it is imperative that we approach it with a sense of inquiry and a willingness to challenge the status quo. The resources and information necessary to make informed decisions about our children's education are readily available to us. By delving into the works of renowned educators such as John Taylor Gatto and John Holt, we can deepen our understanding of how children truly learn and the impact of the traditional school environment on their psychological well-being.

Reading books like "*Instead of Education: Ways to Help People do Things Better*" opens up new possibilities and encourages us to explore alternatives to the conventional schooling model. It is through this exploration and the active seeking of knowledge that we can make empowered choices for our children's education.

"Ask, and it shall be given you; seek, and ye shall find; knock, and it shall be opened unto you. For everyone that asketh re- ceiveth; and he that seeketh findeth; and to him that knocketh it shall be opened."

In reflecting on the biblical passage, we are reminded of the power of seeking and asking. By actively seeking answers, we are more likely to find the guidance and information we need to navigate the complex realm of education. Our quest for knowledge is not limited to spiritual matters but extends to all aspects of our lives, including the education of our children.

So, I encourage you to embrace your innate seeking nature, to delve into the wealth of resources available, and to take the necessary steps to ensure the best educational journey for your child. Through your pursuit of knowledge and your commitment to their growth, you can create a path that honors their individuality, fosters their love for learning, and nurtures their overall well-being.

In our quest to provide the best education for our children, we often encounter moments of doubt, disconnection, and a longing for a better understanding of their needs and potential. Whether prompted by a gut feeling, a tragic event in the news, or a sense of dissatisfaction with the current state of affairs, we are compelled to seek answers, to find the solutions that will enable our children to thrive.

"Our children are late in everything. They no longer fit the institutions founded for them. In particular they have difficulties in adjusting themselves to school; they have become too immature for it. We usually blame the school, which we are inclined to consider an old-fashioned institution. But the way school now functions is additional evidence of the misunderstanding between young and old. The school is in need of renovation, not a change of nonessentials or of parts, but a renewal of the whole thing. Education as a whole has to

be revised; and if the revision is to be effective, it must be nothing less than a total renewal of educational methods, which - as the recent serious attempts at renewal indicate - will be so radical that the slightly older teachers will observe these changes with wonder and will not feel at home with them, even if they do not doubt their necessity and agree as to their effectiveness. For it is clear to anyone who has anything to do with children and with education that something must happen. Ever more children are experiencing serious difficulties during the first few years of primary school. Ever more children remain apart from what is being taught during a good part of the years they go to primary school. Schools are haunted by the ghost called Alexia, one of the family of ghosts to which infantile autism also belongs. It is quite clear that this situation cannot be allowed to continue."

Van der Berg's insightful observation highlights the growing mismatch between our educational institutions and the needs of our children. The call for a total renewal, a radical transformation of educational methods, resonates with the recognition that something must change. Increasingly, children face difficulties in adapting to the traditional school environment, and it is evident that the existing system requires significant renovation to meet their evolving needs.

"Education is knowing where to go to find out what you need to know; and its knowing how to use the information you get."

Education, as William Feather aptly expressed, is not merely about imparting information but also about knowing where to find the knowledge we seek and how to effectively utilize that information. It is a dynamic process that requires ongoing exploration, adaptation, and a willingness to challenge established norms. The information I share with you today is intended to empower you on your journey of discovery, to equip you with the tools to navigate the complexities of education and make informed decisions for the benefit of your child.

We must acknowledge the haunting presence of challenges like Alexia[3], a condition that

---

[3] Note: Alexia (from Greek (a-), meaning "absence of, without", and (lexis), meaning "word") is a brain disorder in which a person is unable to understand

affects the ability to comprehend written words. It serves as a poignant reminder that education should cater to the unique needs and diverse learning styles of each child. As we confront such realities, we are driven to question and reimagine the educational landscape, seeking innovative approaches that can bridge the gap and ensure that every child has the opportunity to flourish.

By offering this information, my aim is to provide you with a starting point for your exploration, to ignite a sense of curiosity and an awareness of the need for change. It is my hope that you will delve deeper, seek additional resources, and engage in meaningful discussions about the future of education. Together, we can pave the way for a transformative educational experience that honors the potential of every child and fosters a lifelong love of learning.

---

written words. It refers specifically to the loss, usually in adulthood, of a previous ability to read.

The New Paradigm

There are various alternatives to traditional schooling that offer different approaches to education. Each alternative is unique in its philosophy and methodology, catering to the diverse needs and preferences of families. These alternatives include homeschooling, unschooling, hackschooling, free schools, democratic schools, Sudbury schools, Waldorf schools, and many others.

Homeschooling allows parents to take on the responsibility of educating their children at home, tailoring the curriculum and learning experiences to their child's individual needs and interests. It provides flexibility and the opportunity for personalized instruction.

Unschooling takes a child-led approach to education, emphasizing self-directed learning based on the child's interests and curiosity. It promotes natural learning through real-life experiences and encourages a child's innate desire to explore and discover.

Hackschooling is an innovative approach that focuses on creating a customized education, combining traditional academic subjects with practical skills, real-world experiences, and mentorship opportunities.

Free schools and democratic schools emphasize self-governance and participatory decision-making, involving students in the democratic process of the school community. These schools foster a sense of autonomy, responsibility, and engagement in the learning process.

Sudbury schools and Waldorf schools offer alternative educational philosophies. Sudbury schools prioritize self-directed learning in a democratic setting, where students are responsible for their own education. Waldorf schools follow a holistic approach, emphasizing experiential learning, artistic expression, and a nurturing environment.

The key is to make an informed decision based on your unique circumstances, values, and the needs of your child.

"Learning is the beginning of wealth. Learning is the beginning of health. Learning is the beginning of spirituality. Searching and learning is where the miracle process all begins."

– Jim Rohn

Reflect on what you believe is essential in an education, consider the resources and support available to you, and explore the various alternatives. Engage with other parents, educators, and professionals in the field to gain insights and gather information. Ultimately, you have the opportunity to choose the educational path that aligns best with your vision for your child's future and provides them with the preparation they need to thrive in the world.

Learning is indeed an inherent instinct that belongs to the individual engaged in the process. It is a remarkable privilege and a fundamental human right. Genuine learning emerges when it is self-directed and personalized, shaped by the unique qualities of the learner. Attempting to impose knowledge upon someone is as futile as trying to make a horse drink water against its will, for true learning requires active engagement and personal ownership.

The act of thinking and reflecting is crucial in internalizing knowledge, allowing individuals to make it their own. This process of independent learning brings manifold benefits, nourishing the mind on various levels. It fosters critical thinking, creativity, and a deep understanding that transcends rote memorization. When learners actively pursue knowledge and construct meaning for themselves, they embark on a transformative journey that shapes their character and expands their intellectual horizons.

It is essential to question our unwavering confidence in knowing what is best for others, particularly when visionary thinkers and luminaries of the past have cautioned us against such certainty. Albert Einstein astutely recognized that education can often hinder genuine learning, as it tends to impose predetermined structures and limit individual exploration.

Peter Drucker, a renowned management guru, emphasized the lifelong nature of learning, highlighting the vital task of equipping people with the skills to adapt to a rapidly changing world. Drucker also humorously noted that obsolete subjects are sometimes enforced as required courses, highlighting the flaws in outdated educational practices. And Rabindranath Tagore, a Nobel laureate, urged us not to confine children's learning to our own experiences, as they are born into a different era with unique perspectives and possibilities.

Quotes, like condensed bursts of wisdom, offer profound insights to ponder and contemplate. They serve as powerful reminders of our innate potential and can help realign our thoughts and actions. Including inspirational and empowering quotes in a personal collection provides a source of guidance and inspiration, encouraging us to challenge the status quo and embrace the wisdom of those who have come before us.

In his book, *Learning All the Time*, John Holt beautifully captures the essence of how children truly learn and grow. He emphasizes that when a child is engaged in something they are deeply passionate about, their potential for growth is boundless.

"A child only pours herself into a little funnel or into a little box when she's afraid of the world - when she's been defeated. But when a child is doing something, she's passionately interested in, she grows up like a tree - in all directions. THIS is how children learn, how children grow. They send down a taproot like a tree in dry soil. The tree may be stunted, but it sends out these roots, and suddenly one of these little taproots goes down and strikes a source of water. And the whole tree grows."

Rather than confining themselves to narrow confines or restricting their curiosity, they expand in all directions, much like a tree reaching out in search of water. This natural process of learning and growth is a testament to the innate potential within each child.

It is truly liberating to accept this truth and let go of the outdated notions and practices that have proven to be detrimental to genuine learning. As we delve into research and gain a deeper understanding, we realize the damaging effects of conventional approaches that limit children's natural instincts and curiosity.

We are undoubtedly living in a time of rapid change, where the knowledge and skills acquired today may become outdated in the near future. Embracing this new paradigm requires acknowledging the evolving nature of our world. Children who are given the freedom to pursue their own interests, often labeled as rebels or troublemakers, are the ones shaping the business structures of this new era. Visionary individuals like Steve Jobs and Richard Branson exemplify this unconventional approach to learning, paving the way for transformative change.

The advent of the internet has provided an unprecedented platform for young entrepreneurs, enabling them to create social media technologies and make significant contributions to the digital landscape. Established corporations are increasingly recognizing the value of these innovative minds, seeking out young talent who have harnessed the power of viral YouTube videos and employing them as consultants. In this shifting landscape, traditional educational credentials and degrees are being challenged, and the youth are being entrusted with the responsibility of solving complex problems and driving technological advancements.

In the current landscape of change and innovation, corporations are recognizing the unique talents and perspectives of young individuals who have made a mark through viral YouTube videos. These companies are shifting their focus, valuing the problem-solving abilities and fresh ideas of these young creators over traditional qualifications and degrees. This shift in hiring practices signifies a departure from the conventional notion that formal education is the sole measure of competency. The future holds promise for those who embrace new avenues of learning and adapt to the evolving demands of the world.

"In times of change, learners inherit the earth, while the learned find themselves beautifully equipped to deal with a world that no longer exists."

The insightful words of Eric Hoffer above, remind us that in times of change, those who are open to learning and growth are better equipped to navigate the shifting tides, while those who cling to outdated knowledge find themselves ill-prepared for a world that has moved beyond their expertise.

Our education systems, once heralded as pillars of knowledge and progress, now face challenges of obsolescence and dysfunction. Many schools have become rigid and oppressive, resembling prisons rather than nurturing environments. Children are expected to passively accept what is presented as truth and world view, with limited room for questioning or critical thinking.

"We don't need no education We don't need no thought control No dark sarcasm in the classroom Teachers leave them kids alone. Hey teacher, leave them kids alone!"

–Another Brick in The Wall, Pink Floyd

Pink Floyd's lyrics from "*Another Brick in the Wall*" echo the sentiments of disillusionment with the education system, expressing a desire for freedom from thought control and an acknowledgment of the stifling environment that restricts individuality and creativity.

The current state of schools serves as an analogy for the broader challenges faced by families in raising children and guiding them towards productive adulthood. The experience of school offers valuable insights into the difficulties encountered in fostering independent thinking and nurturing the development of fully alive individuals.

Peter Block's words emphasize the power of asking good questions to unlock deeper understanding and a more vibrant existence. Unfortunately, our educational systems often fail to encourage such inquiry and instead prioritize conformity to standardized protocols and tests. This environment instills fear and restricts opportunities for experiencing the profound journeys of self-discovery and personal growth that can lead to being fully alive.

It is essential that we challenge the status quo, ask the necessary questions, and explore alternative approaches to education that prioritize individualized learning, critical thinking, and the holistic development of young minds. By doing so, we can create a future where education truly empowers individuals to navigate an ever-changing world and live lives of purpose and fulfillment.

It is clear that the old-school model of schooling is becoming obsolete in the face of this rapidly changing world. The future holds immense opportunities, and embracing the potential of individualized, self-directed learning is crucial for preparing our children to thrive in the new paradigm.

'The pupil is thereby schooled to confuse teaching with learning, grade advancement with education, a diploma with competence and fluency with the ability to say something new. His imagination is schooled to accept service in a place of value. Medical treatment is mistaken for health care, social work for the improvement of community life, police protection for safety, military poise for national security, the rat race for productive work. Health, learning, dignity, independence and creative endeavor are defined as little more than the performance of the institutions which claim to serve these ends, and their improvement is made to depend on allocating more resources to the management of hospitals, schools and other agencies in question."

–Ivan Illich

As a radical home and unschooler, I must confess that my opinions are inherently biased, shaped by my own personal experiences and extensive research. I recognize that this book reflects my unique perspective, and I encourage readers to approach its content with an open mind and critical thinking.

I implore you to take a moment to consider the ideas I present, even if only temporarily. It is commonly assumed that children are the ones in need of help within the educational system, but I challenge this notion. Instead, I propose that it is the parents who require assistance and support.

It may be shocking to consider, but I firmly believe that parents may suffer from the same afflictions as the schools they subject their children to. By highlighting the potential detrimental effects of institutionalized education, I hope to provoke a reevaluation of long-standing assumptions.

It is crucial to approach this book with an understanding that my views represent only one perspective among many. As with any historical analysis, it is important to critically assess the biases inherent in the author's viewpoint. My intention is to inspire readers to engage in thoughtful reflection and to question the roles parents play in shaping their children's educational experiences.

School serves as a child's initial encounter with one of many bureaucratic institutions, such as the military, the media, the consumer society, the political party, and the religious establishment. I understand that this assertion may challenge established beliefs and provoke discomfort.

Take a moment to pause, collect your thoughts, and consider this perspective. It is crucial to approach these ideas with an open mind, as there are potential solutions that can benefit not only your child but also yourself. The first step is to acknowledge that the information you have been presented may be misleading or incomplete. Embracing this notion may initially appear radical, but deep down, I believe you resonate with it.

The classrooms and schools of today bear little resemblance to the ones we remember from our own education. It is essential to acknowledge that the system itself is flawed and in need of significant reform. However, please remember that you are not broken in any way by recognizing this truth. In fact, by embracing this new understanding, you have an opportunity to contribute to the changing world around us.

Consider this book as an invitation to explore alternative paths and approaches to education. By joining this conversation, you become an active participant in shaping the future of learning.

Ultimately, I aim to encourage readers to embark on their own intellectual exploration, to challenge established conventions, and to arrive at their own informed conclusions.

It Is Their Time Now

We indeed live in an extraordinary time where the principles of quantum physics remind us of our ability to shape and create our reality. With this understanding, it is crucial that we imagine and envision the best versions of ourselves and our children.

What children truly need is not just new curricula, but access to the real world. They require ample time and space to reflect upon their experiences, engage in fantasy and play, and derive meaning from them. They benefit from guidance in the form of advice, roadmaps, and guidebooks that assist them in navigating their own paths and discovering their own interests and passions.

Children are born with an innate and powerful desire to learn, and it is our responsibility as parents and educators to nurture and sustain that desire. It should be the focus of continual assessment, as it is the foundation for their growth and fulfillment. Sadly, too many children leave traditional schooling with little to show for their time, feeling alienated and ill-equipped for the real world.

In a rapidly changing world, we cannot predict the specific changes that lie ahead, and our own rigidity and attachment to outdated ideals hinder our ability to provide meaningful guidance. It is time to let go and recognize that this is their time—the time for the next generation to lead, learn, and explore. We must step aside, supporting and empowering them as they navigate their own paths and seize their own opportunities for growth and success.

As parents, our role shifts from ownership to fostering strength and trust within ourselves, allowing our children to venture forth with confidence. We must speak to them as the leaders and visionaries they are, treating them as ambassadors in this world we have created, inviting them to improve it and make it their own.

Indeed, it is their turn, their time to shine, and it is our duty to be present, supportive, and ready to provide resources and open doors for them. Let us embrace this new paradigm of parenting and trust in their ability to shape their world and contribute to its betterment.

I find it fascinating to examine the profound impact our actions and behaviors have on the learning and development of children. One remarkable piece that captures this sentiment is Dorothy Law Nolte's renowned poem, "*Children Learn What They Live*," published in 1954. This thought-provoking composition serves as a poignant reminder of the significance of our awareness and presence in shaping children's experiences.

Nolte's poem delves into various values that shape a child's upbringing, offering profound insights into how these values influence their growth and understanding of the world. It highlights the notion that children are constantly absorbing information from their surroundings, and it is our responsibility as adults to play an active role in nurturing their learning and development.

Children Learn What They Live

If children live with criticism,
they learn to condemn.

If children live with hostility,
they learn to fight.

If children live with fear,
they learn to be apprehensive.

If children live with pity,
they learn to feel sorry for themselves.

If children live with ridicule,
they learn to feel shy.

If children live with jealousy,
they learn to feel envy.

If children live with shame,
they learn to feel guilty.

If children live with encouragement,
they learn confidence.

If children live with tolerance,
they learn patience.

If children live with praise,
they learn appreciation.

If children live with acceptance,
they learn to love.

If children live with approval,

they learn to like themselves.

If children live with recognition,
they learn it is good to have a goal.

If children live with sharing,
they learn generosity.

If children live with honesty,
they learn truthfulness.

If children live with fairness,
they learn justice.

If children live with kindness and
consideration,
they learn respect.

If children live with security,
they learn to have faith in themselves and in
those about them.

If children live with friendliness,
they learn the world is a nice place in which to live.

As I delve into Nolte's work, I am struck by the timelessness of her message. It serves as a timeless reminder that our words, actions, and attitudes have a profound impact on the young minds around us. The poem invites us to reflect on the values we embody and the lessons we impart to children through our everyday interactions.

Examining Nolte's poem from a historical perspective, it becomes evident that the concept of shaping children's experiences and fostering their growth has been a fundamental aspect of human society throughout time. Whether it be through formal education systems, societal norms, or familial influences, the impact on children's lives cannot be understated.

In a world that is constantly evolving, it is imperative that we recognize the importance of our role as educators and caregivers. We must strive to embody the values that we wish to instill in the next generation and create an environment that nurtures their curiosity, empathy, and resilience.

Nolte's poem resonates with the idea that children are not only passive recipients of knowledge but active participants in their own learning and development. It underscores the significance of our words and actions in shaping their worldview and nurturing their potential.

As I reflect on Nolte's words, I am reminded of the power we possess as individuals to make a positive impact on the lives of children. It is through our conscious choices, genuine presence, and unwavering support that we can create an environment where children can thrive, learn, and grow into compassionate and engaged individuals.

Nolte's poem serves as a timeless reminder of the profound influence we have on the lives of children. It calls us to be mindful of the values we embody and the lessons we impart, acknowledging that children are constantly learning from the world around them.

I know it sounds obvious, but you must realize – truly realize - that your children reside in your care, and it is through your actions and guidance that they absorb the essence of their surroundings. They rely on your trust, knowing that you will provide them with the very best of yourself. It is within this trust that they cultivate the confidence that the decisions made on their behalf will serve them well as they transition into adulthood.

Reflecting upon this, one must question whether they are consistently conscious and aware of their role in shaping their children's lives. What transformations must one undergo to ensure that their children are exposed to the finest elements of the world? Can one truly comprehend the profound gift that their children offer, acting as catalysts for personal growth and the liberation from stagnant beliefs? Are parents fully present and appreciative of their children's presence and the wisdom they impart?

Gratitude should permeate one's being, acknowledging that these sentient beings have chosen to be present in this era, entrusting the responsibility of their upbringing to you. It is an invitation to transcend personal limitations and rediscover the joy of play, for it is through play that individuals flourish the most.

Understanding this, how can one ever speak to their child in a condescending manner? How can they imply that their child is lacking in some way, whether it be intelligence, stature, ability, or any other measure? Such notions undermine the inherent worth and potential of the child.

Instead, it is crucial to foster an environment that embraces the child's innate qualities and encourages their growth. Embracing their uniqueness and supporting their journey allows them to flourish and develop into confident and capable individuals.

Your child is capable, and wonderful, and wired with all they need to make it in this world. All they seek from you is unconditional love and closeness.

By acknowledging their presence and cherishing their contributions, parents can create a nurturing space that cultivates a sense of self-worth and fosters the belief that they are indeed enough.

In essence, parents must embrace their role with deep awareness and mindfulness, recognizing the immense impact they have on their children's lives. By doing so, they empower their children to embrace their true potential, fostering a harmonious and transformative parent-child relationship. Let us strive to be the guardians who uplift and inspire, guiding our children on a path of self-discovery and growth, ultimately enabling them to navigate the world with confidence and resilience.

Children thrive when they are allowed the freedom to engage in independent play, free from unnecessary interference or patronizing gestures. Granting them the space to explore their surroundings and make their own decisions fosters a sense of trust and self-assurance. It is important to refrain from intervening and saying phrases such as "do you want me to help you with that?" as it can frustrate and disengage the child from their play. Just as we would feel unsettled if someone intruded on our work, children too desire the autonomy to engage in their own activities.

Respecting their need for independence in play also extends to the belief that play holds significant value in their development. It is through play that children acquire essential life skills and cultivate their imagination and creativity. Contrary to previous beliefs that emphasized the supremacy of formal schooling, we now understand that play is an integral component of a child's growth.

As Albert Einstein famously stated, "*The only thing that interferes with my learning is my education.*"

Play, therefore, should be regarded as the vital work of children, always.

It is paramount to be mindful of the words and actions we direct toward children, ensuring that we do not undermine their sense of self-worth. Even seemingly innocuous comments and expressions can impact a child's perception of themselves. Unfortunately, many parents unconsciously engage in either permissive or punitive interactions. While permissive approaches dismiss responsibility, blaming and punishing tactics undermine a child's confidence. It is essential to recognize that there is another way—a more respectful and empowering way to communicate with children.

The solution lies in treating children as equal human beings, offering them information, and allowing natural consequences to unfold. By adopting this approach, we acknowledge their innate social nature and their thirst for knowledge. Just as we would communicate with an adult coworker or friend, we can engage in open and honest conversations with children. Avoiding blame and excessive praise, which can be equally damaging, we provide them with straightforward information. And when appropriate, we allow natural consequences to occur, providing valuable learning experiences.

Living by example is crucial. Consistency between our words and actions is essential for establishing trust and credibility. It is not a matter of some designated quality time but rather an embrace of an all-encompassing approach. By committing to these principles and embracing open communication and trust, we create an environment where children can thrive, continuously learn, and develop a strong sense of self.

Do not be overwhelmed by the thought of making changes, but rather consider how you can reconnect as a family unit. Embrace shared mealtimes, outings, and errands as opportunities to bond and explore together. Ask questions, delve into the "why" behind things, and seek out new adventures. Make a commitment to befriend your child and spend quality time with them, much like you would with your friends. Reject the notion of segregation and separation and recognize that children are just as human as adults, capable of experiencing and participating in various activities.

I have always taken my children to diverse events and cultural experiences, such as workshops, seminars, theaters, operas, and museums. Rather than crowded "children's days," opt for quieter weekdays when you can have the space to yourselves. Enjoy each other's company and cultivate genuine liking and unconditional love. Reflect on your own actions and ensure that you serve as a clear role model for your child. If you have faltered in this aspect, it is never too late to adjust and be more mindful.

Now is the time to act, to set a new course, and navigate uncharted waters. Nature has designed us to continuously learn and grow, and in doing so, we often thrive and find safety. Stepping outside the confines of the box is not scary; it is liberating, expressive, and joyful. Breathe freely and invite your child to join you in creating adventures and exploring new possibilities.

Sit down together as a family and discuss ideas, formulate plans, and create a vision board that represents your desired life. Commit to this vision and take small steps each day to move closer to your goals. Share with your family that you have gained insights and envision a better way of living and ask for their help in making this shared family dream a reality. Expect children to do the right thing, and they will often rise to the occasion. When you ask for their help, they are usually eager to contribute.

I understand that you may feel overwhelmed, lacking support, or disconnected from your child. In those moments, reach out to the Universe, voice your desires aloud, and gradually communicate them to your family members. Rising to this challenge may seem daunting due to fear of the unknown, but rest assured that light awaits on the other side. I have counseled families who have faced similar circumstances, and although this may be the most difficult stage, the rewards that await you are worth the effort. Trust that you can build the family life you envision and watch it manifest before your eyes.

I encourage you to turn to the Source and seek the strength to overcome any fears and seize this opportunity. When feelings of overwhelm arise, break them down into small, manageable steps. You will be surprised at how much easier it is than you anticipate.

"To attract joy and create more success, try doing less but doing it with more enthusiasm."
–Phillip Humbert

Imagine how your life will transform in the next six months, a year, or even five years if you implement the information I have shared today. Envision the relationship you desire to have with your child. Is it aligned with the vision you held before they were born? Embrace the possibility of creating that wonderful connection.

We all sense that time is passing swiftly. One year from now will arrive sooner than we realize, so focus on taking one day at a time and one small step forward. Remember, even a small step for an individual can be a giant leap for the collective.

Be prepared to make sacrifices and let go of things that no longer serve you. Purge the baggage and release beliefs that hinder your progress. Take the opportunity to slow down and reconnect with yourself and your family. It's time to recharge, rebuild, and find peace. As Mother Teresa wisely said, "*It's better to sweat in peace than to bleed in war.*" Recognize any inner conflicts you may have experienced as a result of disregarding your natural parental instincts. Release any blame or regret, forgive yourself, and exhale the past.

Remember, this moment is all that exists—the present. Embrace your presence in the here and now, and let it guide you on this transformative journey.

In this precious life we have been given, there are no second chances, only the present moment. The world we live in is in a delicate and uncertain state, and the future is no longer guaranteed.

So I ask you, what are you waiting for?

Your children are eagerly waiting for you to step into your destined role as their guide and supporter. They believe in you, and I believe in you too.

The question that remains is, do you believe in yourself?

It is time to take the first step.

The Author

Kytka Hilmar-Jezek stands as a highly accomplished author, renowned for her influential books that have left an indelible mark on readers. With a focus on parenting, education, entrepreneurship, and natural healing, her extensive repertoire of over twenty-five thought-provoking works has earned her widespread recognition, including a place in the Revolution in Education Hall of Fame.

Kytka's passion for education shines through her books, which boldly challenge conventional schooling paradigms and stimulate discussions on alternative approaches. Notable titles such as "The Smartest Kids Don't Go to School," "The Smartest Kids Learn All the Time," and "The Smartest Kids Know School Stinks" offer fresh perspectives, urging readers to question traditional norms and embrace innovative methods of nurturing children in the technological age.

Her debut book, "Reiki for Children," quickly soared to become a global bestseller in 2001, resonating with professionals in the field who employ it as a valuable resource in teaching children. Expanding her healing-focused publications, Hilmar-Jezek has authored works like "Raw Food for Children," "Eat the Light: The Raw Food Diet as a Spiritual Practice," "The Ultimate Beginner's Guide to Reiki," and "The Rainbow Tower," a captivating exploration of Chakras designed for young readers.

Kytka's engaging books consistently enlighten, inspire, and challenge readers on controversial and thought-provoking subjects related to health and wellness, parenting, spirituality, and education. Through her publishing houses, Distinct Press and Czech Revival Publishing, she actively promotes diverse voices across various literary genres, fostering a platform for aspiring authors to share their unique perspectives. With her remarkable versatility, she has ghostwritten over 200 books for clients worldwide and translated more than 100 books from the Czech language.

Kytka Hilmar-Jezek's journey as an accomplished author and book editor is marked by an unwavering dedication to exploring unconventional approaches to education, parenting, health, and personal growth. Her thought-provoking books, advocacy for diverse voices, and commitment to preserving cultural heritage have made a profound impact on the literary world. By delving into her works, readers embark on a transformative journey that challenges norms, inspires critical thinking, and fosters positive change in their lives and communities.

Outside her literary endeavors, Kytka finds joy in various ventures, such as her contributions to TresBohemes.com, where she has penned numerous posts on Czech culture. Her commitment to preserving cultural heritage is further evident in her work preserving old photographs for The Photo Vault and curating items for The Czech Museum. Most of all, she loves to read on lazy afternoons, snuggled next to her Shiba Inu, Richard.

Learn more at kytkajezek.com.

www.ingramcontent.com/pod-product-compliance
Lightning Source LLC
Chambersburg PA
CBHW032037080426
42733CB00006B/107